M000227505

TO FREE

THE

CAPTIVES

TO FREE
THE CAPTIVES

A PLEA FOR THE AMERICAN SOUL

Tracy K. Smith

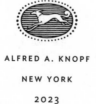

ALFRED A. KNOPF

NEW YORK

2023

LIBRARY OF CONGRESS CATALOGING-IN-PUBLICATION DATA
Names: Smith, Tracy K., author.
Title: To free the captives : a plea for the American soul /
Tracy K. Smith.
Description: New York : Alfred A. Knopf, 2023.
Identifiers: LCCN 2023001898 (print) | LCCN 2023001899 (ebook) |
ISBN 9780593534762 (hardcover) | ISBN 9780593534779 (ebook)
Subjects: LCSH: Smith, Tracy K. | African American women
authors—Biography. | African Americans—History. | African
Americans—Social conditions. | United States—Race relations.
Classification: LCC PS3619.M5955 Z46 2023 (print) | LCC PS3619.
M5955 (ebook) | DDC 818/.603 [B]—dc23/eng/20230420
LC record available at https://lccn.loc.gov/2023001898
LC ebook record available at https://lccn.loc.gov/2023001899

Jacket art: *Sea Saga* by Melissa McGill
Jacket design by Janet Hansen

for Uncle Richmond

We need to lose the world, to lose a world,
and to discover that there is more than one world,
and that the world isn't what we think it is.

— HÉLÈNE CIXOUS

When I found I had crossed that line, I looked at
my hands to see if I was the same person. There was
such a glory over everything; the sun came like gold
through trees, and over the fields, and I felt like
I was in Heaven.

— HARRIET TUBMAN

CONTENTS

TRAIN OF SOULS

3

THE FREE AND THE FREED

37

ONE MORE SUNNY DAY

82

SCENES FROM A MARRIAGE, OR:
WHAT IS THE AMERICAN IMAGINATION

127

SOBRIETY

174

THE NORTHERN TERRITORY

216

CODA: UP AHEAD

256

ACKNOWLEDGMENTS

261

TO FREE

THE

CAPTIVES

R ed dirt. Pine needles and leaves. Trucks and trailers nestled under trees. The steep peak of a church roof. A trailer's rusted eaves. Veins of road, like pale rope afloat on green sea. Railroad tracks running south, north, away. Dark water and a creek's muddy banks. The surface of a place shimmers in rain, shivers in wind.

By what rite might I enter in?

One way of describing what I'm after is to say that I am searching for the soul-family from whom I descend. Because I have been living a long time now with the dead, who refuse to abandon me. Often, it is my deceased parents who arrive, through tumult and tedium alike, to counsel and console. *Buy a new car,* my mother advised only recently. *Don't pour another dollar into that old Land Rover. Get out in front of the problem. Get something sturdy and affordable, the biggest Toyota you can find.* I was standing in my kitchen in Massachusetts, looking out at a row of tall trees that twisted and shimmied in late-autumn wind, when the thought planted itself in my mind, practical and direct. It interrupted some other thing I had been in the midst of thinking. Days later, the old white SUV in which we had been shuttling our children for nearly a decade finally gave up the ghost. But my mother had warned us. And, fortunately, we'd heeded her advice.

My father doesn't speak so much as lean in close offering to ease me of a burden. One whole year, as I listened over and again to Otis Redding preach and plead and get down on his knees with his voice, I felt my father's presence beside me, guiding me to the story of an entire generation striving gorgeously through setbacks lined up like bowling pins by a nation's innumerable hands. And I wasn't any longer aching, affronted, alone. I was alive and continuing, just as my father all his life had been. I was aligned with a tireless tradition.

As the daughter of Black Alabama Baptists, I was given the language of the soul in childhood. The soul—my soul—is indomitable, I was taught. No one but I myself can deny or diminish it. To accept such a thing is the opposite of escape; it is to assent to an everlasting purpose, a cosmic responsibility.

As a child, I encountered evidence of the soul all

around me. Soul food. Soul music. The soul cry only Jesus could pacify. To bear witness to the soul was to attest to something eternal in me—in us and what contained us. It even made idiomatic sense to me that Saturday mornings were devoted to the R&B music TV show *Soul Train,* just like Sundays were set aside for churchgoing. We were soul people, believers in the soul. And Black people were the first folk I knew who invoked the soul constantly. Not with fear, not with threats of condemnation, but in outright joy—mirth even—as though what bolstered this facet of us was, in part, our laughter. Black people falling out in glee, and Black people falling out in religious ecstasy, were two versions of the same thing. Proof of the undying and holy in us.

It is no mystery to me where such a preoccupation would have originated. For my parents and their kin, born into a nation intent upon their diminishment and inured to their dying, the soul stared out from unblinking eyes with the assurance of continuance. *I matter,* it said. *Never mind what you attempt, I will last.*

When I was young and both my parents were still alive, our vocabulary for the soul originated with them. I used and internalized it, but seldom did it fall to me to add to it. Older now, with aches and burdens of my own, I return again to the soul with a new determination. I return seeking connection to the train of souls—my parents, grandparents, ancestors, and guides—who might help conduct me through the din of human division and strife.

<hr />

I find my father's name, and those of his brothers, sisters, mother, and father, in the 1940 Census. They live in Washington County, Alabama, in the town of Sunflower. A warm rush of feeling floods my chest when I see or say *Sunflower, Alabama.* I don't know the Sunflower my father knew, but my love of my father, and my gratitude for the nurturing by which his body and spirit thrived there and grew—that is what the place-name *Sunflower, Alabama,* has long instilled in me.

My father passed away in 2008, but I feel him even now calling my attention to a heron over a pond, or a woodpecker battering a tree. My father's soul—his unfettered energy—revels in all the same things that captivated him when he lived in the body I knew. And so it is easy for me to imagine that same energy soaring over the woods in Sunflower almost a century ago, skimming the rooftops of that red-dirt town, its patchwork of fields and furrowed farmland like a quilt pieced together by hand, before deciding it is a farmer named Eugene Smith and his wife, Rosetta, to whom he will arrive as the ninth of ten children—like a tiny comet—on Halloween 1935.

The family farm feels large and safe to my father, who

at the time of the census is not yet five years old. The barn and vegetable plots and the long rows of a peach orchard are the first places where the wonder of life greets him. Piglets grow into hogs, acorns into saplings. A peach pit dried on a windowsill promises to sprout, one day, into a tree laden with fruit. He plays in the grass, disappears under the vast canopy of a family of pines. To run, to ponder, to lie distracted on this land is what freedom feels like to a child, though where I say *land,* my father's word is likely *home.* Maybe he knows that nature is the source of this safety and splendor. Nature, heeded and tended by the men and women in his family, is also the source of health, sustenance, and security, the amalgam of which must simply be *happiness* in his four-year-old vocabulary.

As a boy, my father races down Monroe Lane to the blacksmith shop run by his grandfather James Sigmund Brown, a deacon and associate pastor at Little Sunflower Baptist Church. My young father is full of questions. He loves gears and levers, sharp angles and smooth planes. He is allowed to crank the wheel that churns the bellows while his grandfather renders red-hot metal into ax-heads, hammers, the headboard of a child's bed. When my father fetches his grandfather tools, his small legs hurry so as not to miss the molten metal cooling into heavy solid work, worth. Work, too, is a font in my father's young mind. It yields purpose and dignity. He learns this from the men in his family whose hands build, prune, and plow, providing. And from the women—his mother, aunts, and cousins on adjoining properties—whose sewing tables, cake savers, and kitchen gardens sustain and delight. These quiet lives, small from the outside, are nevertheless essential to an enormous enterprise. What is it called? My father can't yet say. But it reverberates in the music of the everyday. A spade sunk into earth. The cadence of new logs split. Footsteps in a pantry. The whir and scrape of a whisk.

As he ventures farther, my father's experience will begin to assure him that his people are stewards not solely of the known creature that is family, but of a larger animal called History.

It is a lesson I, too, am endeavoring to learn. Right now, in sifting through census columns and draft notices. In asking these and other artifacts to attach themselves to the voices and stories—the hands and hearts—I trust and love. I am seeking to affirm for myself, at a moment when the large dark form of our nation's past seems to be ever at our heels, snarling and baring sharp teeth, that history is not something to run from. No. It has held us, birthed and nursed us. And if its wild heat is not content to recede, perhaps it makes sense to stoop down, gather it up in my own hands, and carry some piece of it—some wriggling kit or pup—forward.

What have I been given, what do I now hold, that can be of further—even of urgent—use?

<hr/>

These acres north of the fork in Garland Road—these lanes and fields where my young father roams—are known as Browntown, for the many members of the extended Brown family who have made their home here over time. The patriarch, my father's maternal great-grandfather, Richmond Brown, was born in Alabama in 1846. The 1900 Census lists him as a laborer, and his wife, Emma, born in 1848, as a cook. It is difficult for me to zero in on the circumstances of their births, given the resources I have. Owing to slavery—the institution that would likely have defined the parameters of their life until Emancipation—it is probable such details will remain a mystery. Even if my great-great-grandparents were born free, in all reality slavery would have limned the scope of their opportunity. I long to understand how they perceived that borderline, and whether or when the hazard of it appeared to recede; it would mean something to be offered a record of their thoughts, wishes, and memories. But as far as I know, there are no letters or diaries attesting to these and other things; neither could read or write, the census says.

What I do know, what the documents consent to tell

me, is this: Richmond and Emma raise their large family in Sunflower. Emma has told the census agent that she is mother to sixteen children, fourteen still living. In 1900, six sons and daughters—Botany, Stephen, Amanda, Kate, Kellie, and William—are dwelling in the family home. Sons James, born in 1869, and Richmond Jr., born in 1872, are heads of their own households on adjacent land. Who is missing? When were they born? To what did they succumb? Were any sold away (a common consequence of a barbarous institution)? If so, where did they go? Whom did they become? Certainly they loved. Amid everything else, they surely must have tasted joy. How I long to kneel alongside the brawl of their voices, the throes of their living. But when I try piecing together the branches of my kin, what I find at so many turns are questions. The absence and silence into which they have been made to disappear arrives to me now as grief. But there was—there surely still somehow is—more. If regarded properly, if approached with the right questions, what might my seeking yield?

What were you looking for? Why did you leave? Who hurt you? Whom did you hurt in turn? What did you take? What were you given in your time of need? Did you believe what they told you about yourself, about them? What went missing? Whom did you trust? When did you realize you were tired? When it got too heavy, what did you let go? What was the most cutting, the cruelest thing you said? Heard? Were told? Was there music? By whom were you fed? When your body shook, when your sight clouded over, when you fell to your knees, what was the name you cried out? Who held you? Was it wilderness to which you were taken? A city? Were there other miracles? Who died? Who fled? Whom do you visit most now in dreams?

The conundrum of history is that we think it is behind us. But if it came first, doesn't that mean it should be up ahead, turning back now and again to see if we are keeping up? Which version is true? And what does it mean when we are told, as often we are in this country we share, to *Move on, Get over it, Put the past behind us?* Where are we going? Whence have we come? Can we yet train ourselves to admit the past more fully and honestly? If so, what might we learn about this thing we call freedom?

Frank Smith, my father's paternal grandfather, was born in Mississippi in 1862 or '63. He was a trapper in a coal mine in Empire, Alabama. When I land on this detail, just this tiny fragment of his story—his name, his approximate year of birth, and his occupation—light floods a room in my mind I had not previously imagined to exist. A trapper, I learn, sits beside the wide plank doors in a mine, opening them so that the laden carts might be allowed to pass, and then closing them back to divert dust and flammable gas. In my great-grandfather's time, trappers were sometimes children. They sat listening for signals that would lift them out of their tedium. Their patience was paramount; if they dozed or grew distracted, disaster could ensue. My father's grandfather had done this dangerous, tedious job, a job that a child could do.

According to the 1920 Census, Frank Smith can neither read nor write, but all six of his children can—even six-year-old Floyd, for whom my father was surely named. Very soon, my grandfather Eugene, the eldest of Frank and Lucinda Smith's children, will marry Rosetta Brown. *Daddy* is what his ten children, my father included, will call him their entire lives. Even now, *Daddy* is how my uncle Richmond—my father's sole surviving sibling—refers to him when I phone with my many questions about these census names and dates.

After one phone conversation, my uncle calls right back to add, *Daddy served in France in World War I.* In my uncle's voice, this information is private, a detail by which he seeks to make his father more real to me. But when the digital archive of military records, which has no investment in my curiosity, yields up my grandfather Eugene Smith's draft card, affirming that he enlisted on June 5, 1917, it is as if my grandfather becomes realer not just to me, but to our country's history.

Assigned to Company D of the 340th Labor Battalion, my grandfather sailed aboard the USS *Huron,* which embarked "for Overseas" from Newport News, Virginia, at 3:00 p.m. on June 18, 1918. He and the other Black soldiers awaiting departure would have been housed in the all-Black Camp Alexander barracks, named for Second Lieutenant John H. Alexander, the second African American graduate of West Point. Lieutenant Alexander is at most nineteen in the photo where

SECOND LIEUTENANT JOHN HANKS ALEXANDER, CIRCA 1883

his hair has been brushed into soft waves and parted to the side. There is something about the downturn of his mouth that gives me the impression of a great blast of commotion going on inside his mind.

I search up images of Black soldiers from my grandfather's time. Corporal Benjamin Harrison Splowne, who enlisted in the army on the very same day as my grandfather, stands staring, it seems, into my eyes.

CORPORAL BENJAMIN HARRISON SPLOWNE,
CIRCA 1917

Something about his gaze makes me believe I can almost register the rise and fall of his breath, the barest hint of movement in the buttons running down his chest. I'm reminded of something my son once tells me when he is very young and unable to fall asleep: *You have to be scared to be brave.*

In the photograph of my grandfather from this time, he is standing before a stone building or wall, shoulders

EUGENE SMITH, CIRCA 1917

squared, lips closed but not firmly set. The top portion of the image has been handled to faintness, or else was underexposed to begin with. The right side of my grandfather's face—and with it his hint of a mustache—threatens to vanish, like a face in a dream. Folded, cradled, prayed over, this record of a single instant of 1917 is creased and fissured. But I am there with him, and he is here with me when I lay eyes on the daylight dappling my young grandfather's warm brown knuckles.

The young men in the war photos all seem as if something within them is deciding. Young men, hats atilt, not sure what they are sailing into. Young men posing at downtime on a heap of rubble, bricks fallen into a low mound, smiling like war is a kind of school. The young men in one photo are four blacksmiths at work in a tent in France. One stands with his back to the camera, facing the left edge of the frame, off toward the place where daylight appears to be rising or else sinking down behind trees. In the middle distance, a young man looks toward the camera as if held in thought. He smooths a new horseshoe against a whirring file. A dark horse toward the right of the frame waits. The young man in an apron holds the horse's hind leg, hammer in hand, face so gentle I think he must be the best at what he does, *tink-tink*ing in the final nail, or else lifting one out with a tenderness steeped in love.

BLACKSMITH SHOP, 366TH INFANTRY,
SERQUEUX, HAUTE-MARNE, FRANCE, AUGUST 11, 1918

Does anything watch us back? I wonder. Not the men in pictures like these, whose living defied the bounds of any photo's frames. No, I want to know whether there is some other presence that lingers in the wake of these and other lives. Something that grazes us with its gaze, seeking to be heeded or helped along. Something arriving, like light from across the expanse of space, to tell us who and what we truly are, and where or by whom our better efforts are required. Is this why we matter to the past, if indeed we do?

A commonly cited motivating factor leading Black men to enlist in World War I is hope. They are hopeful that, in helping to defend democracy in Europe, they might prove their—our—loyalty to this nation. They pray their service might vanquish the ugly contradiction of racism and second-class citizenship at home in this bastion of freedom and democracy. According to U.S. Department of Defense archives, the majority of Black infantrymen are conscripted to labor and engineering corps. They clear roads, raze forests, raise bridges. Some, like the all-Black 369th Infantry, also known as the Harlem Hellfighters, enter into combat with consummate heroism, pushing back enemy lines to such an extent that they are celebrated as seminal to the success of Allied forces.

Someone has written *HERO* in the upper right corner of Corporal Lawrence Leslie McVey Sr.'s portrait. He wears the same wool tunic-collar coat as my grandfather and Corporal Splowne, but around his waist is a canvas cartridge belt from which hangs a short sword in its scabbard. McVey's right hand is flat, as if at attention. The first and second fingers on his left hand straddle the scabbard: a habit from long acquaintance. His hat is set at a young man's tilt, and he is, to my eyes, very young. McVey was a member of the 369th Infantry. According to the Smithsonian's National Museum of African American History and Culture, which holds McVey's photos and wartime artifacts, the 369th was

CORPORAL LAWRENCE LESLIE McVEY SR.,
CIRCA 1914–1918

assigned to France's oversight owing to racial tensions within the U.S. military.

McVey was seriously wounded in the final weeks of the war, while leading his squad in an attack against

German machine gunners in Séchault, France. For his heroism, he was awarded the Purple Heart, the French Croix de Guerre, the Legion of Honor, and Inter-Allied Victory Medals from both France and the United States. France's Victory Medal, which hangs from a rainbow-striped ribbon, is to my eyes the most pleasing. Winged Victory is depicted on the obverse, arms outstretched, sword at her side. On the back is the phrase *La Grande Guerre pour la Civilisation.* I can almost feel the object's heft in my palm, can almost allow myself to claim a portion of the pride it must have conferred. I imagine these Black soldiers receiving theirs and for a time feeling nearly repaid for something. *The Great War for Civilization . . .*

How long would it have lasted, the feeling of being deemed a hero, indispensable to the fate of his nation? How soon upon returning home would McVey, and Black veterans like him, have been reminded that there is always a war brewing in America. A war fought in train cars and restaurants. In classrooms and theaters. Under the breath, under the collar. In the words of W. E. B. Du Bois, *not everywhere, but anywhere.* If I wish to lay claim to a portion of these men's pride, what vigilance—and what grief—must I also accept as mine?

In a photo from soon after the close of the war, McVey is back home in New York. He sits cross-legged on a beach in a striped bathing costume. He smiles broadly,

CORPORAL LAWRENCE LESLIE McVEY SR.,
CIRCA 1920–1930

holding both arms outstretched toward the camera so that his hands in the foreground bid us toward him. In the photo's bottom margin, in blue ink, someone has written:

Daddy—

I want to honor this young man, courageous on the front lines of France, the returning veteran whose celebrated heroism inevitably receded against the demands of day-to-day necessity. He assented to the duty and the dignity of providing for a family. He found work with the Pennsylvania Railroad—likely, given hiring trends at the time, as a station porter or in a railway dining car. He raised a family whose love for him, and whose hope for this country, led them to offer up his story to the larger body of American history.

On September 30, 1968, at age seventy-one, Corporal Lawrence Leslie McVey Sr. was attacked and beaten to death in a New York City park. History is here beside us when we consider such a fact. History, arriving to tell us this one thing more about the centuries-long war in which countless have fallen, are falling still. History, imploring us to confront what has been hammered into us about which lives matter, about what it is that some are entitled to and others are expected to fight or even die for. History arrives to remind us where and by whom our better efforts are sorely required.

History *arrives*? Better to accept that it is never gone, despite our insistence to file much of it safely away, out of sight and mind.

I taught for a decade and a half at Princeton University. Time and recognition are two things universities offer their faculty, who, with enough of these commodities, foster a civil—even a cordial—culture. But my first institutional disappointment, slight as it may be, returns to me now as I contemplate the promise and the freight of the historical archive.

It was an early afternoon in summer, and I was accompanied by three guests from Emory University, whose Stuart A. Rose Manuscript, Archives, and Rare Book Library was in the process of acquiring my literary papers. At Emory, I'd sat poring over Lucille Clifton's poems in typeset or handwritten form, marveled at lines struck through for deletion, pondered the additions of sometimes a single word by which a draft was made to spring into Art. There was something comforting about thumbing through the great writer's desktop day-planners stuffed with check stubs, errand lists, and marked year upon year with a reminder of her June birthday. At Emory, I'd also once bent over the page upon which Seamus Heaney had decided that his own poem "Tête Coupée," whose speaker contemplates the bog-preserved remains of a beheaded girl, ought rather to be named "Strange Fruit"—at which instant the murder and erasure of its Iron Age subject is thrust into dialogue with the living specter of racialized violence in America.

The life force rising like breath off paper pages. The

dark smudge of oil where a thumb once lingered. The moisture droplets—water? tea? tears?—smudging a column of words so that the ink is burbled, blurred. Pages of text written in such haste that there was no time to lift up the pen, no attempt to distinguish one word from another. It is intimate. Enrapturing. An encounter in which you are allowed almost to brush knees under the table with the work's maker. It makes you feel large, as if you, too, are held in a reciprocal regard. And also small, a mite upon the massive page of time.

When my guests and I approached the rare books and manuscripts admissions desk at my own institution, we were regarded with suspicion. What were we looking for? By what authority did we seek to enter? It wasn't enough to explain that I was a member of the faculty. Did this extra scrutiny have to do with the size of our party? Was it merely how the clerk had been trained to perform her job, to protect what she had been told was at once vulnerable and formidable? I felt profiled, dressed down, dismissed. We weren't admitted. We were sent away with instructions on how to petition for access at a later date. In this anecdote, Princeton as an institution is not unique or even particularly pivotal. Similar exchanges occur all the time—*not everywhere, but anywhere*—and especially in spaces where, consciously or not, the framing of the past serves to shore up and justify existing hierarchies of worth, power, and belonging.

When we speak of the violence of the archive, we are generally referring to the silences and erasures from which we might seek to rescue stories of lives written off as marginal or slight. We are shedding light upon the flattening perspective of power, which tromps through the historical record, endowing some lives with innate value, and dismissing others outright. But there is another violence I have been made to recognize: one seeking to convince some that the archive is not for them, that it is maintained for the benefit of an authorized few into which they—we—by dint of who we are or how we approach, do not figure. It is a form of intimidation akin to being followed in a department store: *Can I help you? Can I help you? Can I help you?* But we have business here. There are stories and lives to liberate—stories and lives that can liberate us. All of us.

I have turned now to the archive for help gathering up a fuller picture of my grandfather, who'd have held me in his arms, or sat me on his knee, toward the end of his life when I was just a baby. At the same time, I am contemplating this single member of my family as a means of engaging more mindfully—more heartfully—with our nation's history. Had there been time for Daddy Gene to walk down France's storied *rues* and *boulevards*? Had he heard American jazz played there by Black men like him? Was there a Frenchwoman who smiled and let his arm brush hers while that music unlike anything else in the world caught them up? I've read that the racial tension between Black soldiers and whites could be set to boiling by an act like that. And also that some Black men, soldiers and artists alike, returned from France confessing they'd felt freedom there for the first time in all their lives. Fragments like these, drawn piecemeal from the recorded experience of veterans my grandfather's age, augment the terms of my imagining. They assure me that my grandfather brought his heart and imagination with him to the war. He dreamed. He longed. He escaped the constraints of his racialized reality for moments and hours at a time before being made to squeeze back in, feeling at once larger and more keenly aware of his confines. In this way, history enters my body, too, taps my own feelings, ceases to be clinical. By which I mean, it becomes more like life itself. Just as my grandfather, by way of those other young men who help me conjure him, ceases to be a figure from the sepia-tinged past or even solely a family member, and becomes a young man on the threshold of his life.

Often enough, hunting through archival records, I feel as though I am traipsing through a dark mine with only a flickering lamp by which to see. When, in an effort to determine my grandfather's exact whereabouts after his return from France in 1919, I locate his name on the 1920 Census, it takes me a moment to realize that I have merely doubled back to the same bend in the tunnel where I first stumbled upon his father, my great-grandfather Frank Smith, the coal mine trapper living with his family in Empire, Alabama. He is still as if waiting there by the wide plank doors, alert, listening. *Here I am,* his spirit calls to mine, the way the spirits of departed loved ones are said to return in order to shepherd the newly deceased into the afterlife. Now I see that he has told the census worker that his eldest son, my grandfather Eugene, who is twenty-seven in 1920, works there with him as a driver. And yet—Eugene also appears in the 1920 Census as residing in Sunflower. He and his wife, Rosetta, own their home (the census indicates it is *free* rather than mortgaged) and each is employed. Eugene, the head of this household, has told the census worker that he is a teamster *driving a dam.* Rosetta is a seamstress. There are no children as of yet. They live in the same district as Rosetta's father and kin. I don't know how to account for what appears to be a hiccough in the archive. How can my grandfather have

lived in two separate households in two separate coun-
ties at once, in one an unmarried son and in the other a
newlywed husband?

And then I remind myself that the census—that history in general—is a game of telephone.

Eugene is not yet *Daddy Gene* in 1920, and his wife
is not yet *Mama Rose.* They are a young couple starting
married life together. Rosetta's brother, Wash Brown,
has also just returned from World War I, where he
served in Bordeaux. Maybe the men, both born in the
same year in the same small town, have known each
other all their lives. Or maybe they became close overseas, with Wash telling Eugene about his younger sister
back home, the one with the wide smile and the long
black braid. It is hard for me to locate Wash Brown in
1920, but by 1930, he is back in Sunflower, married to a
woman named Cornelia. The Brown and Smith households are listed one next to the other on the census grid.
Maybe the hardscrabble necessity brought on by the
Great Depression forced families to gather the patchwork of community around themselves more tightly.

The name of another neighbor, Simon Tricksey Sr.,
jogs my memory. A letter he sent to Alabama governor
Benjamin Miller lives in digital form in the Alabama
Department of Archives and History. It is handwritten
in pencil by Tricksey, who would have been thirty-one
or so at the time, younger than my grandfather by almost

a decade. By now the stationery—a lined memo pad—has yellowed, but the voice penciled onto the page feels ever urgent; it tells a story the census withholds, isn't designed to tell, or simply has no way of knowing, about life in Sunflower during the Depression:

Sunflower, Alabama
July 7, 1933

Governor B. M. Miller

Honorable Sir,

I am writing you concerning my [Reconstruction Finance Corporation] Job. It is so many meddlers here. Very near all of the colored folks have been cut off. Some who hasn't got bread, and at the price now, will not be able to get it and have large families.

I was cut off this week. I didn't know any thing about it until I was told today. I do think that since I'm of age the folks should have asked me, of my condition with out taking some one else's word. I have a family of 5 am aged, and blind mother to help care for. She is in her late 70s. My wife has a very aged cousin, of whom we have to help care for, since she hasn't any husband or children or any close Relatives to depend on.

We only get $1.00 per day and groceries are unreasonably high. .35 per pk for meal. Flour .65 for 12 lbs. Meat .15 per lb for common kind of dry salt.

It hasn't been a man on the job that worked any better than I. Either has it been a time that I've been late going on the job.

I feel like I haven't been treated just fair and have such responsibilities on my self and several others with large families. It's only a few colored people on the job now.

Now if I have said anything to cause any offence I humbly ask for appol.

Kindly let me hear from you soon regarding this matter. Since I need some help or a job. Will work any place. I owe a store acct now.

Humbly yours,
Simon Tricksey Sr. (Col.)
Sunflower, Ala.

In his pressing appeal, Tricksey is identifying an abrupt shift in circumstance. He's also bearing courageous witness to the feeling—no, the certainty—of having been dealt an injustice. The economy is in collapse. Everyone is feeling it, but he feels singled out, laid off from a job he's good at, and with no warning. And it's not just him. *Very near all of the colored folks* are in the same boat. In a time and place where Jim Crow laws mandate Blacks' deference to whites, Tricksey dares sign his name to a letter that is essentially a grievance. What if it is no accident that Blacks, especially in the South, are being pushed to what we might think of as the front lines of the struggle? A place with no cushion and few to turn to for explanations. A place where they themselves become the cushion—the buffer—keeping whites in the same general communities from losing even more than they've already lost, which is more than they or anyone else can afford to. As much as Tricksey's letter is a plea for his job to be reinstated, it is also a petition to be treated fairly. He seeks to be understood. Is that the problem, that state authorities do not understand what his community is up against? Just in case, he lays out the terms of his and others' circumstance and requests the courtesy of a straightforward explanation. *Kindly let me hear from you—*

The reply from the governor's office dated July 25 reads:

Dear Sir:

Governor Miller has referred to me for attention and reply your letter with reference to reconstruction finance corporation job.

The amount allowed to Alabama by the

*Reconstruction Finance Corporation has been
reduced. We are working now to get more funds.*

    *You should talk over with the people in charge of
the matter in your county your situation and I am
sure they will give careful consideration to it.*

Yours very truly,
John H. Peach
Legal Advisor to the Governor

The two concrete facts that Peach consents to divulge
are that funding has been cut, and that he and his asso-
ciates are *working now to get more.* But for whom? And
by when? In comparison to the life force still palpable
in Simon Tricksey's letter—where I can discern the
cadence of breathing, of a heartbeat, of hand gestures
stirring up air—John H. Peach's reply reminds me of
certain bots I have encountered. There is nothing
kindly about it. How perfectly Peach manages to com-
mit to nothing: not regret, not sympathy, not even hope.
Tricksey's letter is full of lives: *meddlers, colored people,*
infirm relatives, hungry families. Peach, on the other
hand, conjures up a vague body of *people in charge of
the matter.* They have no names. There is no specific
office where they can be found. How can they give careful consideration to something that will likely never

make it to their desks? Do they have desks? Does Peach even believe—or does he simply imagine—they exist?

An institution—a government, an industry, a bank, a church, a university—is not a family. But like parents and loved ones, institutions purport to be invested in our care. As with kin, we are bound to them. They keep track of where we live. They know our needs, recall our setbacks. Some institutions make it possible for us to have and to hold, to buy and to sell. A great portion of every institution's rhetoric has to do with its investment in our success. And so it is logical, or even intentional, that our expectations of the institutions most closely touching our lives would have something in common with our expectations of the people we trust and love.

Like my forebears, I also know what it means to allocate part of my earnings toward a mortgage and the support of a dependent family, to be indebted to faceless banks and institutions for whom my identity boils down to credit risk and little more. But compared with Tricksey and my grandparents—even compared to my own parents—my current life is characterized by a moderate luxury. This is no accident. The foundation for my circumstances was laid by their diligence, their selfless providing, their ingenious resourcefulness, and their willingness to risk personal comfort and safety in petitioning for the collective dignity of their entire community. More than capital, these commitments were their greatest currency.

The institutions that have touched my life most consistently, from the time I was an eighteen-year-old leaving home until now, are universities. At a university, the figures responsible for the management of affairs have smiling faces. They express pride in your work. They seek to assure you that with them you are at home. When my peers and I came of age, the first among us to purchase houses or apartments did so with the help of family members. In my case, two of the three properties I have owned were purchased with the help of universities; in this one way, universities have operated for me in loco parentis even into my own adulthood. To thrive at a university is to be held in a position of satisfaction and also indebtedness, to believe that your happiness is intertwined with your ability to do your best work, and—though it is in your best interest to erect boundaries around the sanctity of your time—to harbor the inclination to say yes to what is asked of you. But the nature of an institutional bond is not unconditional.

John H. Peach's limp, circuitous, abstract, half-hearted prose (can a thing be quarter-hearted?) has been carefully crafted to say Something while mostly saying Nothing. Nothing is often enough a preferable alternative to saying, simply, *No*. Nothing is a holding pattern, a cloud passing before the sun. Nothing might, at first, cause the recipient to wait a moment, still believing some benevolent person-in-charge might, like a gust of wind, come forward and clear the obstacle.

The archive offers no indication that the help Tricksey sought ever arrived. Around this same time in the Depression, Wash Brown and Eugene Smith are sentenced to sixty days in jail for obtaining goods under false pretenses. For twenty-five dollars, their sentences can be reduced to twenty days. Are they? I can't tell. I can still hear Tricksey in the background, insisting, *We only get $1.00 per day and groceries are unreasonably high. .35 per pk for meal. Flour .65 for 12 lbs . . .*

But there are other institutions we live with, ones we fashion for ourselves. Forgiveness is one, and the inventive genius by which we improvise our own means of making do. The quilt stitched with a message. The allegiances sworn or born into, by which we hold hands, helping each other move forward and along. Tricksey pleaded with the Alabama state government for a measure of kindness and regard. And when this institution failed him, I imagine he turned to the large family for whom he was responsible, and the wider patchwork of kin encircling them, letting what flowed freely among them carry him through.

Is love an institution? It's often likened to an investment, something that grows over time, bears fruit, yields returns. If nothing else, love is a sustaining force, a source of strength, resolve, and inspiration. Love makes things happen when it seems that little else can.

More than worry, more than necessity, more than need or grief, it is love that I interpret, now, in the many names that recur throughout my father's family line, all the Richmonds and Jameses, the Floyds and Genes, the Roses baptized generation after generation. Love, I believe, is what will wake my father early sometimes during my childhood in California to fill the backyard smoker with a shoulder of pork like the ones lining his father's smokehouse in Sunflower. Love is what will tip us all into laughter over stories from his childhood so long ago. There is no column for Love on the U.S. Census, but it holds the key to some of what I am seeking now in gathering up these names and traces—this evidence—of the people in my father's family.

But for the time being, it is only 1933. My father is ageless still, a soul in space. For whatever reason, he chooses these people in this place, as perhaps once in another life they chose him. He takes it all in. He studies the tradition into which he will descend.

THE FREE AND THE FREED

My father's older brothers Robert and Melvin are nineteen and seventeen years old, respectively, in 1940. Both are described in the census as laborers working forty-hour weeks. The highest grade either has completed in school is seventh. Perhaps they are needed at home on the farm. Maybe the money they can bring in at jobs is essential to making ends meet in a large household. It's possible they leave school willingly, not keen on books. Maybe they already see themselves as adults—men in a house full of little boys and girls—and so they go ahead and do what men of their time believe they must do.

On Valentine's Day 1942, Robert registers to serve in the army. According to his draft card, he has a scar on his left temple. By this time he is twenty-one, divorced with no children. Is enlisting one way of clearing the slate after heartbreak? It pulls him away from a job as a mining machine operator at the DeBardeleben Coal Corporation in Empire, the same mine, now part of a larger conglomerate, where his grandfather Frank Smith had worked in 1920. Enlisting may be an early step in what Robert hopes will be a new chapter.

Melvin has been working a civilian job a few miles south of Mobile at Brookley Field, the new military manufacturing base in the port of Mobile Bay. Erected as the result of a $26 million defense contract, the base has spurred an influx of Black workers to the area; communities pushed by Depression circumstance to a state of subsistence at best and desperation or petty crime at worst are now racing back onto the job market with hope—and hope of relief. *Everyone* is racing to work: women and men, members of Mobile's working class, Native Americans and poor whites from neighboring farming towns jostle against one another in a city suddenly boiling over with resident workers. This circumstance has brought with it new tensions. I've heard of a Black man who had his *head busted wide open* for drinking from the wrong water fountain at Brookley Field. Maybe the threat of such violence strikes Melvin as little different from war itself; on June 30, he enlists. On his draft card, as on his brother's, someone has ticked off the boxes corresponding to Negro (race), Brown (eyes), and Black (hair, complexion).

Are my uncles Robert and Melvin electing to tend the animal of history? Or are they seeking, instead, to flee

Jim Crow, the familiar beast whose job, among other things, is to dispirit and thereby discourage the aspirations of the Black men, women, and even little children within its reach? Understanding what my country demands of people like them—like me—why do I imagine it isn't always a combination of the two? Like their father and mother, and like their younger sisters and brothers, my uncles were born into this nation's long war fought in train cars, classrooms, concert halls— anywhere at all. All are, whether we allow ourselves to realize it or not.

Throughout the summer of 2020, my brothers, my uncles, my sons—all were safe. And yet war raged. George Floyd, Ahmaud Arbery, Rayshard Brooks: in the eyes of our country, were they not my brothers, my uncles and sons? Was Breonna Taylor not my sisters and daughter? Was she not me? These names, these lives, extend from a lineage that has never not touched me. That is what their names remind me, and likewise, what I am made to see in the record of how and by whom each of their distinct lives was stolen. The summer of 2020 affirmed this lineage constantly. It was mine. It would never not be mine. I watched, I grieved. In my grief, I chose to speak. I told white people—we might just as easily call them institutions—that they were guilty. I named what it was they must be willing to put right, to give back.

My error, I now see, had been believing I was Free, that freedom had long ago been won for me. My error was in exercising a freedom I did not, in reality, possess. For in reality, I am not Free but rather Freed, a guest in the places—we might just as easily call them institutions—where freedom is professed. Hence, the many cruel things a few people said. Hence the few true things left unsaid. All those words, all that silence, and how much and how little any of it managed to change.

The Freed—people like me—descend from histories of subjugation. Violence, enslavement, forced migration, and other such acts committed in the names of men, women, and even little children whose freedom has long been accepted as an a priori condition. For the Freed—people like me—nothing that is ours defies contestation. Nothing that is ours has not, at one time or another, been regarded, handled, pocketed, and tossed begrudgingly back by the people presumed to have always been Free.

As natural as it is made to seem, to be Free, as the Free have deemed themselves to be, is not a congenital condition, not a natural extension of innate capacity or earned worth; it is a willful act, a pact with erasure and forgetting. As such, it has long been an occasion for the planting of new flags and the mapping of fresh territory. Occasions on which blood has been shed, as often it has, are converted swiftly into proof that the freedom of the Free must never be contested.

It is hard to touch ground before a priori. When we do, we the Freed are charged with ingratitude, faulty memory, even sedition. How dare we want more than our ration? Would we rather revert to being chattel, mules, nations of children? Was that not, after all, what we were, before being liberated from such conditions by the Free?

It might be easy to read this and think of skin in all the shades, from Black to white. But I would prefer to speak of institutions—societies and organizations, each with its own practices and customs—to which a person might be conditionally admitted. Conditionally, because there is no guarantee that one's welcome will not, from one action, statement, or behavior to the next, be revoked. Conditionally, because one of the chief tenets of freedom, for the Free, is the right to refuse service, deny admission, and otherwise disallow the belonging of anyone at any time who has, for any reason, been deemed unworthy.

Aren't certain households institutions? And likewise, certain hearts? What if memory is an institution? And the American Imagination, which defines the targets of our allegiance, and sets the terms of our belonging—is it not also an institution, with all the privileges and obligations implied therein?

⸻

Like the men of their fathers' generations, Black men and women my uncles' ages bear witness in wartime to the demoralization of the military's enforced second-class citizenship. In 1940, more than twenty years after the victory of World War I, they are still bristling against prevailing stereotypes of Blacks as shiftless, cowardly, incapable, and untrustworthy. Like their fathers and uncles before them, they are betrayed by the policy assigning Blacks to service units rather than combat, and the practice of ensuring that they are never put in positions of authority over whites. More than two decades and a history of worldwide commendation behind them, and still Blacks who do find themselves on the front lines are forced time and again to prove their valor to bigots and naysayers. As had been true a generation before, it is the camaraderie of the affronted which affords Black GIs shelter from the many seeking, as the saying goes, to *put them in their place.*

Racism can't be a surprise to my father's older brothers. The code of segregation has long determined the opportunities available to them and their forebears. The coal mine where my great-grandfather Frank Smith found work, the kitchens where Emma Smith had served as cook, the colored water fountains Melvin would have been required to use at Brookley Field—all of those things and more have been made likely—inevitable, even—by Jim Crow. Jim Crow is the principal force that determined where Eugene Smith and Richmond and James Brown were able to purchase land. Jim Crow is the specter encroaching in small and large ways upon the scope of their autonomy. Jim Crow peers over the shoulder of a state bureaucrat like John H. Peach, just as it directs banks, police officers, bus drivers, and others to do its bidding. The South's Jim Crow laws are the legal mechanism by which the Freed are held apart from and maintained in subordination to the Free, whose freedom in America is respected as inalienable from their very persons. Such laws don't only narrow the psychic horizon of Blacks; they also foster latent anger and resentment in whites by urging them to believe that the integrity of their freedom (uncontested though it may be) depends upon Blacks being put and kept *in their place.* A task like that can be done all manner of ways . . .

Do my uncles fight back against prevailing notions of their inferiority, and if so, how? By speaking up? By doing their stoic best despite the ebb and flow of anger, resentment, and despair? Where does that stew of feelings leave them? What do they carry back into civilian life after the war? My instinct is to trust that they've had a lifetime to learn the danger of fighting back, bristling, demonstrating rage or resentment of any kind. They know how to carry these feelings within, where—powerful as they may be—they won't tip my uncles into greater precarity. They claim absolution, knowing the shame of racism does not belong to them. They heed the soul, with its assurance of continuance. This is labor they perform every day almost unconsciously, labor into which they were born. There is something about this dynamic, I suspect, that both is and is not intended to be gotten used to. Even for the Free, it requires the constant labor of exercising, while simultaneously appearing to deny, the power by which their freedom, or what they perceive it to be, is reified.

Everyone, you see, is laboring. Some labor to stand up again from blow after psychic blow. Others labor to contort their faces or even just their minds to fit bigotry's pinched confines. Even those who insist they are exempt from burdens such as these must nevertheless labor not to see the distinct lanes and deep grooves all in America have, over centuries, been corralled into. Even now, we tend to such work daily—all of us—consciously and otherwise.

The region of my mind calibrated to decide when it is wise to step into a crosswalk—the one that warns me to wait until the approaching vehicle has slowed with the unmistakable intent to stop—is accompanied by another instinct. *Wait,* it commands. *Confirm the driver's assent to respect your person. Nod. Wave. Linger until there is the deliberate meeting of your gaze.* Now and then, I come into conscious awareness of how long it takes for these circumstances to align. Other times, I am the driver lifting my hand, nodding my head, vowing in this way to let another dark person cross safely in my path. Oftener still, I am the driver brought to an abrupt halt by a pale pedestrian striding freely from the curb without the slightest seeming glimmer of doubt.

<hr />

Across the United States, job-placement programs, housing and small business loans, and tuition assistance—aka the GI Bill—promise returning World War II veterans an on-ramp to the middle class. But for Black veterans returning to lives in the South, the majority of these promises go unmet. Oversight of job-placement programs in segregated cities like Mobile is handled by Veterans Affairs administrators who are the Southern, white products of Jim Crow (*You should talk over with the people in charge of the matter in your county your situation and I am sure they will give careful consideration . . .*). Black men and women returning from the war are routinely passed over for the very jobs they are, thanks to their military training, newly qualified to perform. Instead, they're offered positions as janitors, cooks, housekeepers, workers in meat packing plants. And the low-interest loans guaranteed by the government are still granted (or denied) by private banks and lending services whose practices and preferences are little different now, where Blacks and credit are concerned, than they were before the war. Even with tuition assistance, Black veterans won't be admitted to colleges and universities that haven't yet been integrated. Meanwhile, Historically Black Colleges and Universities, underfunded since before the war, lack the capacity to accommodate the many veterans seeking an education. In other words, the more things change, the more they stay the same. By far, most Blacks who imagine the GI Bill might offer a way around second-class citizenship are quickly made to admit Jim Crow's intractability anew.

Robert and Melvin have been working since they were teens, and work is what they return to in peacetime. Robert claims a job with the U.S. Postal Service, steady work that qualifies him for a pension. He marries, starts a family. Melvin finds work at what my uncle Richmond describes, simply, as *a plant*. In old photos, my father's brothers are smiling, handsome, happy. Young men in windbreakers leaning against potbelly cars. Should it undermine their happiness to also acknowledge that chapters of their lives illustrate how the divide between the Free and the Freed is maintained and fortified? By

MELVIN, MARTHA, EUGENE, HARVEY,
FLOYD, RICHMOND, AND ROBERT SMITH, 1970

and large, and no matter who we are, can't the same be said about chapters in all our lives?

By 1950 Simon Tricksey Sr. and his wife have left Sunflower. They are members of their daughter Rose's household in Mobile. Their son-in-law, Jasper, is a contractor. Simon has picked up work as a gardener in a nursery. And it is a help, surely, to have grandparents in a house with three children filling the rooms with commotion, and with hope. It is easier for a young mother to think her own thoughts when there are more eyes on her little ones, more hands tending to all the things always needing to be done. I imagine the grown folks' gentle laughter sifting through open windows after the children have been put to bed. It rhymes with the nighttime chatter from my own childhood.

When my father graduates from high school in 1953, rather than seeking work at Brookley Field or DeBardeleben Coal, or even the U.S. Postal Service like his uncles had in the decade before, his plan is to go north to Detroit. He'll stay with his older sister Mattie and her

FLOYD SMITH, EARLY 1950S

JOHNNY AND MATTIE, EARLY 1950S

husband, Johnny, a World War II veteran, until he can find his footing. A job in the auto industry must appeal to the young man with the fascination for beautifully made things, for shining tools and smooth gears. Even if he doesn't luck out right away at an auto plant, he's sure to believe someone with his aptitudes might find work as a mechanic, or mechanic's apprentice. I bet his head is as full of dreams as the city, when he reaches it, is teeming with chaos and possibility.

The father I knew loved neat spaces, green spaces, peace and quiet. Order appeased him. Disarray made him anxious, uneasy. And so I can only imagine the shock—the queasy perplexity—that must overtake him upon his arrival at the Greyhound bus terminal in Detroit's Skid Row. When he looks up from the sidewalk, his gaze is snagged in a web of traffic lights and trolley cables. Bars, hotels, pawnshops, and loan offices line the sidewalks, which are so busy with panhandlers and police officers, with working men and women, that he can't afford to look up anyway. My father has never seen this many signs and kiosks, so many lights flashing in broad daylight. Is he light-headed? Frightened? Does he worry he's made a mistake? And even so, is there something in him that bucks with haphazard hope?

In 1950, Blacks made up about 16 percent of the population in Detroit, largely in densely populated Black Bottom and Paradise Valley, neighborhoods with cheap rents and where they weren't barred from the chance to own homes of their own by redlining and racially discriminatory covenants—the legal agreements preventing non-whites from owning property in specific areas of an ostensibly integrated city. By the time my father arrives, Black Bottom is almost completely gone—buildings razed and residents displaced to make way for a freeway. I wonder if he stays in one of the small wood-frame houses in Paradise Valley, which is quieter now, too, than in its heyday. But even with most of the big music venues and hotels shuttered, the sound of so much late-night activity, so much raucous hope and need, is a shock to my father's senses. He's up at night tossing and turning, half wanting everyone else to shut up and go to sleep, half hoping he'll soon have a paycheck to cash so he might be out there living it up alongside them. Before ATMs, before cell phones, before online job listings, my father arrives in Detroit with a quantity of cash he'd have been warned to guard closely and make last. Once, twice at most, he may phone home, conscious of the extravagant expense of long-distance calls. Mornings, evenings, he busies himself hunting through newspaper want ads like these:

Attention, Workers!
We need 5 men part time to sell used cars. White or Colored. No experience necessary. We train you. Car furnished and $50 a week guarantee. If you qualify. See Mr. Howard, Northwest Motor Sales, 20000 Livernois. DI 1-1451.

BOYS—Two, white, work Saturday with other students; satisfied about

$1.50 hourly. 8:30 a.m. Saturday only. 1446 Majestic Bldg.

COUPLE—Colored: live in; wife acts as housekeeper and care of 2 children, husband do part time chores. LI 5-0925

MEN for inside cabinet finish: steady job for right men. Mr. Richards. 19113 W. Warren.

FIELD'S EMPLOYMENT—Colored laundry, dry-cleaning help, cooks, maids couples, janitors: day work TR 3-7770.

Decades away, in a future my father has no reason yet to imagine, I will haunt his kitchen, as he must in 1953 haunt his sister's, hunched over newspaper columns whose tiny type advertises: *WANTED, Immediate openings, Excellent opportunity.*

Zigzagging the city after job leads, my father meets discouragement. Ford has downscaled its workforce. Slowly, steadily, factories are beginning to move out of the city. With fewer job prospects in general, Black job-seekers like my dad have a hard time catching a break. My father hates to talk about racial discrimination. Segregation has been an everyday reality his whole life, closing doors, ushering him toward what's left over after whites take what they regard as their due. But plenty has kept him standing tall. The warmth and support of going to school with friends, neighbors, and kin. The care and encouragement of teachers who recognize something in him and tell him as much, praising his discipline, attesting to his potential. Wholesome, abundant food grown on his family's own parcel of land. Nature's peace and beauty. Kin on their patchwork of neighboring lots. Such things bolster my father's soul, minister to his pride. They make a way out of what it might be easy to mistake for no way.

Here in Detroit, my father is harangued by the day-and-night racket of car engines and police sirens. The air's not clear. Buskers, hawkers, everybody carries on as if content to put their business right smack in the street. He's out the door early looking for work, not wanting to appear shiftless, not wanting to be a burden. The only lead he's found, the only opportunity that doesn't threaten to vanish when he gets within reach, is with the Detroit Police Department. But he's been warned about the police. He's seen them lining up Black men, patting them down. The first time he helped his father slaughter a hog, it brought him to his knees choking back vomit. He's not a farmer. He doesn't know what he is yet. But he will not be a cop. He cannot bring himself to join their ranks.

For the moment, he gives up. Rides the bus back to Alabama. Thirty-six hours, give or take. I don't know the first thing my father does when he gets home, but I imagine he is greeted by his mother, whose love lifts him up, making it impossible, for the moment, to slump. *Baby,* I know she whispers, *you have a home here, no matter what.* That, or something like it.

And how must Sunflower feel to him now? He wants to call it heaven—the woodpeckers, pine trees, gurgling creeks. Fresh air, wide-open sky. He wants to claim this peace. But he's been somewhere now, seen so many people willing to do just about anything to make do, to get by, to scratch and scrape for barely enough. A desperate, run-yourself-into-the-ground kind of life. Maybe he'd be living that way, too, if the right doors would have let him through. He's been someplace, and as awful as it felt, as mean and loud and hard as it had seemed, it causes him to wonder new things.

Knowing my father, knowing his love of books, his head for numbers, his sense of joy and wonder at the workings of nature, I am certain he thinks about college. My mother—whom he met in high school and to whom he's been writing letters this whole time—has been attending Alabama State, an HBCU in Montgomery. Were he to follow her there, or follow her example and matriculate elsewhere, he'd be the first in his immediate family to earn a college degree (he's already only the second son to finish high school). But something keeps him from choosing this path. Is it money? Tuition sure does feel like an obstacle. So does the question of rent and living expenses away from home. In the 1950 Census, Daddy Gene's employment status changed from *Farmer* to *Unable to Work.* My father must be feeling pressure to contribute to the household, to help keep the family—and even the extended patchwork of kin— afloat. At the very least, he can't bring himself to be a drain on others. In his way, he is responding to the same demands that led his brothers Robert and Melvin to leave school all those years ago.

Oh, my young father! I'm old enough now to regard him as the child that he is at eighteen. Old enough to want to assure him there is nothing he can't do or be. But I recognize the look in a young person's eye when there are obligations they must obey, allegiances that outweigh just about every other dream, or threaten to. Eyes that have decided. Eyes that are deciding. Eyes that believe they must somehow decide.

My father enlists in the air force. In the photos from this time, he's a young man with a thoughtful, faraway gaze, the one often reading a book or cradling a tobacco pipe. Sometimes he seems to me to be fixed on the future, other times the past. Either way, there is an elsewhere, a space just his that he carries within. He packs up, ships off to basic training in New York. The way he'll infuriate his children on weekend mornings, shouting upstairs to demand that we *Jar the ground!*— The way he will be satisfied with nothing but immaculate neatness— His standards so rigid and high it seems there is nothing good enough to please him entirely— All of this, I imagine, he begins to learn in basic training.

From just about the beginning of his career in the air force, my father takes classes. At first it is *Basic Electricity. Wave Generation. Aviation Communication Systems Theory I* and *II.* And then *Management Training. Principles of Sociology. History of American Civilization. Political Science.* Semester upon semester of classes offered by the air force and via correspondence and at community colleges near just about every base where he is stationed. In my senior year of high school, after my father has returned to civilian life, I take a pair of these classes myself: *Art History* and *Music Appreciation,* taught in classrooms at Travis Air Force Base, where perhaps my father has once sat. I wonder to what degree these subjects satisfy the hunger to learn and to prove that I suspect he has long possessed. For my part, they stoke the wish I've nurtured since my oldest sister, Wanda, left home for college: to race into the faraway world. For my father, who manned the prow of our large family, attending college classes for a few hours each week might have been his way of doing the same.

My parents are married in November 1956 in my mother's grandmother's house. A story my father once told me, after my mother had passed away, is that when they arrive at the hotel my father has reserved by phone for their honeymoon—a place he's been advised will welcome them, no problem—the clerk refuses to admit them. *This is no place for negroes,* they are told. As much as you know about segregation, as many times as it's touched you, the blow of discrimination doesn't go away. You talk yourself back up. You put things into perspective. But you've been hit nonetheless. It's no accident. Second-class citizenship does its work over the duration. A large part of this work hinges on the fact that, no matter how much you have been taught by experience to anticipate, the punch still lands, every time. You do and do not ever get used to it. This is part of segregation's insidious design. My parents go elsewhere to celebrate their first night together as husband and wife.

My parents and their growing family go many places together. New Hampshire, Newfoundland, Texas, Nebraska, Massachusetts, Virginia, California. My father serves as an avionics engineer stationed in Thailand during the Vietnam War. So seldom does he tell us children about his work and the travel it requires him to do that my siblings and I come to joke he must be a spy, when in reality our father provides for us silently, bearing his duty with patience and dignity. We have what we need, and often enough what we want as well. Our home life is a well-managed machine that never seems to list or slow.

I remember afternoons at home with my mother in the years before I entered school. Some days my father would drive home for lunch. We lived close enough to

FLOYD AND WANDA SMITH AT SHEPPARD AIR FORCE BASE,
WICHITA FALLS, TEXAS, 1964

KATHRYN SMITH AT ERNEST HARMON AIR FORCE BASE,
NEWFOUNDLAND, CANADA, 1959

the air force base to make this reasonable, though the
visits were necessarily brief. He'd open the door, and
I'd run to greet him, hugging him at the knees. I was
three, four, five. I'd watch him eat, then neaten himself
back up to leave. He wore air force greens or blues and,
some days, a small hat shaped like an inverted canoe.
He carried a hard black briefcase, and sometimes a
canvas satchel of tools. All of it too heavy for me to lift,
though often enough those afternoons I tried.

The Freed know they have been freed by the arrival of
certain opportunities. They integrate communities that

once barred their entry. Their children attend colleges and universities, and go on to enter professions that once seemed out of range. They have earned the right to enjoy these things. They have earned the right to occasional bouts of pride. But there are speed bumps to help ward off their presumption of entitlement, guardrails by which the Freed are discouraged from confusing themselves with the Free.

In 1962, upon the death of Wash Brown, my father's uncle who served in Bordeaux in World War I, his widow, Cornelia, places an application for a veteran's gravestone. In the box where military decorations should be listed, she has written *Victory Medal*. It would have been sent to him by post after the war, with a return receipt for confirmation of delivery.

An official has gone through the headstone application, verifying much of the information supplied by Mrs. Brown. The abbreviation "Hon." has been added to the top of the form in red ink, confirming that Brown's was an honorable discharge. But in the space for honors, a line has been struck through Cornelia's handwriting where she has written *Victory Medal*. The word *None* has been squeezed into the box, also in red. Logically, bureaucratically, this correction clarifies that the French Victory Medal is a foreign honor, not one conferred by the U.S. military. And yet my heart can't help wondering in what spirit this official in an Alabama outpost of Veterans Affairs has sought to set the record straight. If such glib dismissal unsettles me now, how must it have felt to a widow in grief?

When I think of what it means to love a country—to honor, serve, and obey—I begin to suspect that, whether it realizes this or not, America is many times over a widow in grief.

I have inherited several boxes of my father's files. Military records. Commendation medals and certificates. Recently, I've come across a 1974 graduation program for the United States Air Force Senior Noncommissioned Officer Academy. The guest speaker on this day in 1974 was a general who started his career as an aviation cadet in 1942, the same year my uncles enlisted in the army. Like my father and uncles and grandfather, he was born in Alabama. But their paths veer apart from there. After completing a combat tour in Europe, he became an instructor pilot, and commander of numerous squadrons. The verb *command* appears eight times in various forms in his bio. By 1974, he had been decorated with the Distinguished Service Medal, the Silver Star with one Oak Leaf Cluster, the Distinguished Flying Cross with two Oak Leaf Clusters, the Air Medal with sixteen Oak Leaf Clusters, the Purple Heart, and the Republic of Vietnam Armed Forces Honor Medal,

First Class. He is *So-and-So Jr.* Did his father serve in World War I, like Daddy Gene and Uncle Wash, whose draft cards are missing a triangular segment of the lower left-hand corner—the government's way of identifying recruits like them as Black? If so, this man's father—*So-and-So Sr.*—his card would have remained intact.

In an accordion file, I find a form letter dated October 17, 1977 (the day after a surprise sixteenth-birthday party thrown for my brother), indicating that my father owes the military a debt of $1,030.63 for *Overshipment of Household Goods.* The money, the letter announces, is to be remitted by a payroll deduction of $103.60 per month over the next ten months.

Even before I calculate that this proposed payroll deduction is equal to about five hundred dollars per month in today's economy, even before I pore over the columns of money in and money out each month (which leaves less than one hundred dollars' worth of wiggle room for my family back then), I feel my father's panic. I know he feels accused, like he is being called a thief. And I know he feels indicted in another way, too—the way that says, If you were doing better, if you had chosen differently, if the circumstances had allowed for more, this letter wouldn't be a cause for alarm.

I snap to my own still-fresh memory of being blindsided by a titanic tax bill written in the same chilling governmentese—syntax designed to tell you that no justification on your part, no private catastrophe, no emotional appeal, no anything will have bearing upon the government's determination to collect a debt you have allowed yourself to accrue. What does the Bible say? *Give unto Caesar what is Caesar's, and unto God what is God's.* That letter made me feel like a fool for having failed to do either. A similar wave, part failure and part fright, crashes down upon my father on the sunny autumn day in 1977 when the letter arrives.

Tucked into the same file, there is a handwritten draft of my father's reply, and duplicate typed copies of the same. He writes:

I am a career airman.

This debt of $1030.63 arose from the shipment of household goods from Hampton, VA to Fairfield, CA in October 1975. The shipment was considered overweight for my grade.

I was assigned to Langley AFB, VA in 1972, after completing a SEA tour. Upon my arrival at Langley, no base housing was available, which required me to purchase a house on the local economy at Hampton, VA. In 1975, the 314 TAW, of which I was a member, deactivated, and I received a non volunteer assignment to Travis AFB, CA. During the three years at Langley I had accumulated the necessary furniture, appliances and clothing to accommodate my family of seven. The assessed weight of my belongings outweighed the designated limit for my grade, which resulted in the indebtedness to the government. Upon my arrival at Travis AFB there was no base housing available due to renovation. This required me to purchase a house on the local economy at Fairfield, CA. Although the equity received from the sale of my house in Hampton, VA did not constitute a loss, it was not adequate for a down payment on the house purchased here in Fairfield. Therefore, a loan was secured from the Travis Federal Credit Union to accommodate that requirement. I now have five children in school, of whom two are attending college.

The attached AF Form 2451 comprises a summary of my financial status. To be burdened with this additional responsibility would impose a grave hardship which I am financially incapable of enduring. Therefore I respectfully request remission and cancellation of this indebtedness.

We did not have a piano. We did not have a pool table. We did not have a boat. We had a kitchen table and chairs, and a dining room set. We had books. We had a sofa and upholstered chairs. We had some games. We had beds for the seven of us. We had dressers and chests of drawers. We had my mother's old college trunk full of her quilts. We had some saws and tool chests, because the desk in my brother's room, and the coffee table in the family room, and the bookshelves in the downstairs hall were things our father built with his own hands. We had everyday dishes for everyday meals, and my mother's wedding china for holidays. Are these things we ought not to have needed, as the family of a career airman?

My father will never claim discrimination, but it is as if I can hear Simon Tricksey's voice there beneath the words in my father's letter, doing what my father refuses to do—saying plainly and unapologetically, *I feel like I haven't been treated just fair and have such responsibilities on my self and several others with large families.*

Not long after this episode, my father will be promoted to chief master sergeant, the highest rank in the air force for a noncommissioned officer. Had he entered the service through a military academy, or after graduating from college, he would have been on the track to become a commissioned officer, in which case his ceiling of opportunity—let alone the weight allowance given him for moving his family from one posting to another—would have been higher. Would he have been a commander? Possibly. Would he have been challenged, questioned, put in his place, or else simply watched for signs of the traits Blacks are rumored never to shake? It is hard for me to imagine this wouldn't at least sometimes have been the case. At the time of the move in question, which took place in 1975, he was a senior master sergeant, with a weight allowance to match. Are we to take my father's rank and grade—as probable for him as for all the others like him who joined the military as an alternative to middle-class lives kept, for whatever reason, just out of reach—are we to take that as a cap on his lifelong aspirations? Put differently, is rank an official means of keeping a man like my father, from a place like Sunflower, *in his place*? Even if it is nothing but a benign classification, like height or weight, a letter like the one my father received must have reminded him of the limits on what he could reasonably allow himself to hope for, let alone expect.

The military is a meta-institution, a central line of defense for the many actual institutions operating within American culture, and also for the institutional nature of certain regions of the American Imagination. The military reinforces deference to hierarchy; regard for status; respect for the sacrifices returning veterans, fallen heroes, and prisoners of war have made in service to our nation and its ideals. Even today, when so many once-common rules of conduct in contexts from business to politics to love have been bent or blurred or altogether brushed aside (at least for the freest of the Free), the military remains one last bastion of imposed order imploring the rest of us to know the rules to obey. Even if obeisance is a guarantee of at most modest rewards, for some it remains a compelling alternative to the certain punishment awaiting acts of disobedience.

My father's appeal is appended to a letter by his commanding officer, which attests to his character and the good faith of his actions. The captain's letter also makes note of the size of our family, which standardized rank and weight allowances don't seem to take into consideration. This voice of authority validating my father's plea arrives like the Something that never came to the aid of Simon Tricksey a generation before. The animal of history—it is an ancient ox moving slowly on cloven hooves—has journeyed some way, at least. Even so, my father's case and the stress it surely costs him remind me to worry that there will always be circumstances when obedience is not enough of a safeguard (for the Freed, especially) against questions arising from extra scrutiny.

My mother's experience as a military wife reminds me that the policing of a person's aspirations occurs from within as well. My sister Jean remembers how unkindly a group of Black women—wives of other airmen living in our family's vicinity on Offutt Air Force Base in Nebraska—had behaved toward our mother. The gossip, the side-eye, the comments uttered just loudly enough to be heard, all at our mother's expense, though there was nothing logical that could be said to have earned her such treatment. Decades later, in the summer of 1992, our parents take a road trip across the United States and make a stop at Offutt. I understand the urge to return, to behold from the safety of a different life what once felt so large and indomitable, or else small but nevertheless inescapable. By chance she looks up one of the women she remembers from that time and finds her still living nearby. *I don't know why Mom reached out to her,* my sister tells me. *Those ladies were always so mean.* But sitting together all that time later, this particular woman apologizes. *Your home was so nice, your children were so well behaved. We envied you. We thought you believed you were better than the rest of us.* And so their instinct, young as they all were, was to punish her for casting the radius of her dreams a little farther off than they had been told they were allowed to cast theirs. This, too, is a strategy of America's centuries-long war, which demands we fight (in cul-de-sacs, in dining rooms) even against ourselves.

On that same road trip, my parents pay a visit to my brother and me in Boston. The night before they are scheduled to arrive, I set out for my boyfriend's apartment in Beacon Hill from the summer rental I'm sharing with classmates in Somerville. It's hot out, which is why I have decided to *run around half-naked,* as my mother would scoff if only she were to glimpse me. The city is still full of university students, but it's late enough that the streets feel empty. Standing alone at an intersection, waiting for the light, I am hit by a wall of icy fright when a Ford Crown Victoria exactly like the one my parents drive crosses my path. *For a second, I thought that girl was Tracy,* the passengers might say to one another, if indeed they are my parents. I shake the thought from my head and reclaim composure. I cross when the light assures me it's safe. The car, inside of which my parents or someone else's ride, glides farther into the night.

For my part, I am learning how little I knew. It is only now, happening upon my father's files, that I come to recognize the colossal effort by which my siblings and I were allowed to mistake ourselves for the Free.

By the time all four of my older siblings are enrolled in college, our father declines another nonvoluntary assignment, this time in Germany. He leaves the service with the following: a Meritorious Service Medal, a Bronze Star, an Air Force Commendation Medal, an Air Force Good Conduct Medal with five Bronze Loops, a Small Arms Expert Marksmanship Ribbon, a Noncommissioned Officer Academy Graduate Ribbon with one Oak Leaf Cluster, an Army Good Conduct Medal with two Bronze Loops, an Air Force Longevity Service Ribbon with five Oak Leaf Clusters, a National

Defense Service Medal with one Oak Leaf Cluster, a Vietnam Service Medal, an Air Force Outstanding Unit Award, and a Republic of Vietnam Campaign Medal. His military education record spans twenty-four years.

My father looks back with pride on his military career, but he can't dwell on it. He is thrust onto the civilian job market. I wrote a poem about his first post-military job—a contractor position on the massive Hubble Space Telescope project, an operation that spanned from coast to coast across the nation. There was great pride on the part of my father and his colleagues, and there was also enormous stress owing to spherical aberration of less than one-millionth of a meter on one of the telescope's two mirrors. In a group photo of his team, my father stands in the middle and to the right among several rows of men and women. He's about the age I am now, fifty, and wears a turtleneck sweater under a tweed sport jacket. His wide stance is confident, as is his gaze. But the fact that his is the only Black face makes me protective of him all over again. The men who came to our house for dinner now and again were jovial and kind—but who is to say how far the camaraderie of that unit reached? My father never talked about such things with his children. Still, all these years after it is too late to do anything, I worry.

I worry, too, about how much he would have felt the brunt of the world's initial disappointment at the calculation errors rendering the first Hubble images blurry. A 1990 article defending the Hubble and the hope it represents, written by Lennard A. Fisk, associate administrator for Space Science and Applications at NASA, has been distributed to all employees on my father's team; perhaps it has been distributed across the entire project. Fisk assures readers that, even with the aberration, which will soon be corrected, *Hubble still has 100 times greater sensitivity to ultraviolet light than any other telescope, on Earth or in space, 100 times greater spectral resolution, and about the same visible light resolution as a good ground-based observatory.* With corrections, he writes, the device will *achieve every goal set for the 15-year lifetime of the telescope.*

I am writing this within the first few weeks after the launch of the James Webb Space Telescope in 2022, more than thirty years into the ongoing lifespan of the Hubble, which scientists expect will last until 2030, possibly even 2040. I both can and cannot imagine the obstacles to progress my father came up against in his life. Regardless of the role he played in the creation of this device, I claim the enduring worth of the Hubble as a form of victory in the face of any and all naysayers my father was made to brace himself against in his life. This might sound like nonsense to the Free. But how often are the people I've been referring to as the Freed told to look to the heavens—to the moral arc of the uni-

THE HUBBLE TELESCOPE OPTICAL SYSTEM, WITH FLOYD SMITH
IN THE FOREGROUND, FEBRUARY 1986

verse itself—as the site where just rewards and justice await?

All the classes, all the training, all the educational milestones that allowed my father to progress through the ranks in the service, and even to land the job that kept our family afloat for six years after his military retirement—turns out it cost him some effort to petition the Community College of the Air Force to accept his many accumulated credits in fulfilment of an associate's degree. In correspondence dated June 18, 1984, he wrote:

The enclosed transcript satisfies the remaining credits required for my associate degree in Avionics Systems Technology. Due to my retired status, I petition special consideration for reevaluation of my accomplishments, and request a certificate for my associate degree be issued.

Your cooperation in this matter would greatly enhance my quest for future employment.

I cannot tell whether his petition was granted. But I know that even with an AA as his highest level of education, my father would have been at a disadvantage on the job market. Indeed, the truth of this is borne out in 1987, after his Hubble contract is over, when he is deemed ineligible for employment by the U.S. Defense Contract Administration on the grounds of education. At the time, my brother Conrad is in medical school. In three more years, I'll be admitted to Harvard. By every parenting marker, including shielding his children from worry, my father has been a success. But he is back on the job market again; he cannot afford to be judged solely as a father.

I was sheltered from it then, but I have since come to better understand the tireless tradition that is my inheritance. The weight a soul is sometimes asked to bear. It ought to be too much, and yet—how often the soul bears up.

I spent 2020 at home in New Jersey with my family. From March onward, through the months of pandemic quarantine and on into what has been termed a summer of racial reckoning, I taught remotely and served as an academic administrator at the institution where my professional identity had been forged. The terms of my own privilege assured me that I would almost certainly go on living and working in safety. I was an American in the age of Donald Trump; an African American in the age of murderous police brutality against Blacks; a thinking person in a time of massive online outrage, conformity, and misinformation. And yet somehow still I believed myself safe. *Somehow still I believed myself safe?* It startles me to state this fact, though I hope it might illuminate something to describe the nature of the conundrum. Despite my attainment of professional and class standing, despite my service to an institution, despite the fact that I am conscientious and law-abiding—despite all of that, and by mere dint of the fact that I am a member not of the Free but the Freed, I ought to have expected to feel less than safe in my day-to-day living.

Some of my students confronted challenges of their own. One wrote to say he was terrified by the traffic of ambulances he watched from his bedroom window in Washington, D.C., transporting COVID patients. Too many mortalities. The siren wails. The red and blue lights spangling each night. Another sought (and, fortunately, was granted) permission to return to campus from the household where their gender expression made them a target of attack. A handful of undergraduate activists, among the most vulnerable persons in the university hierarchy, chose to address a gathering of faculty—screen after screen of aging faces glaring out from the grid of a videoconference—not with the reverence or adulation our standing has instructed us to expect as our due, but with a list of the ways we, in our positions of relative power, had failed them. They hoped it might illuminate something to describe the nature of that particular conundrum.

Institutional indifference can trip off existential crises. I have witnessed it. In 2020 I endured it. At a university, institutional indifference might take many forms. Performative debates over whether racist speech must be tolerated or even protected. Hesitation to redress comments and actions designed, even unconsciously, to undermine a Black person's sanctity in a classroom or a country or a life. An academic bureaucrat who holds up his hands, telling you that what has been said or written or done to or against you is not—at least not yet—an actionable infraction. For the mind and spirit of the Freed, these are by no means minor setbacks; they reinforce an age-old command: *Know your place. Keep to your place. This is no place for . . .* It is not that we are not, most of the time, made to feel welcome and safe; it is that we are also always braced for reminders that our welcome and our safety are provisional rather than guaranteed.

But imagine if universities, the oldest and most well-regarded of which are drivers of shared culture and collective imagination—imagine if they took to heart the responsibility of ensuring the peace of mind of their most vulnerable students. Imagine if they could bring themselves to comprehend what it means to have surrendered a region of your own psyche for a task that is at once conscious and involuntary; ongoing and sporadic; superficial and soul-deep; an intermittent nuisance from which experience has trained you to bounce back, and a psychic marathon you must run until you drop. And imagine if universities, in setting out to educate a nation, also offered to alleviate from its affiliates the burden of *exercising, while simultaneously appearing to deny, the power by which their freedom, or what they perceive it to be, is reified.*

I spent 2020 at home in the comfort of family. But for how I felt much of that year, I might just as easily have been in my uncles' or grandparents' or some farther-back ancestor's skin, dipping a toe into what has been proffered as freedom, but knowing full well it wouldn't make me free, not entirely.

I think many Black people found ourselves feeling a similar way. Watching ourselves die is always a source of pain. Watching ourselves die while the nation watched, too, at times surprised into outrage, at times bemused, at times moved not to apologize for but to defend the theft of our lives—why should I need to explain that after the initial shock of this pain came a heightened awareness of our ongoing vulnerability? These near daily reminders—daily being the pace of debate around the worth of our lives; daily being the pace of violence against us—fomented in some an age-old resentment, something many of us had gotten good at believing was past the age of best use. But it was useful again suddenly. It was almost consoling to remember that America was not and had never been what we're taught to believe it could be. Against our wishes we built this nation. Against the laws of humanity, our bodies constituted its wealth. We defended it. We petitioned it. And here, I am moved to quote the men credited for founding it: *Our repeated petitions have been answered only by repeated injury.*

If I told you I loved a man who had treated me the way our nation has treated my race, you would tell me to go, to leave, to flee. Black people in America are not fools for love, don't you see? We are the leverage without which there is no such thing as freedom, no evidence that anyone is, or has ever been, or might one day dream of being Free.

The despair of such a realization is difficult to shake. And yet it is imperative to try. By which I mean: my father helped me that year. The knowledge of what he had endured, the challenges and setbacks in the face of near-constant demands. As much as I knew about him, as much as I was allowed to know, he didn't despair. Did he worry? Did he sometimes cry, or ball his hands into fists thinking how hard things sometimes felt? More and more I know he must have. But more often he laughed. He smiled. Sometimes he even sang. He took pride in what he nurtured and made. What he worked hard to earn, he passed down, gave away. Yes, I think maybe he'd have seen freedom that way, as a prize to be shared—and in sharing, multiplied.

What else held me up that awful year? Not an institution, nor the permission institutions seek or purport to confer. Rather, what sustained me was the power made, conjured, and claimed by the people—I've been calling them the Freed—once openly held back from the promise of America's authorized institutions. People who once were officers, owners, commanders of nothing so much as Soul. Faith. Praise. Love. People in whose mouths these were—are—living words, capacities animated and electrified by the opposing poles of their—of our—collective experience. For though we have only ever been freed by men, do you know what we believe ourselves to be? Delivered. Delivered by God.

How many imaginations, hearing such a thing, are apt to cringe at sanctimony, superstition, naïveté? I think I understand why. In this country and elsewhere, religion has long been put to use defending the indefensible. For some, it has naturally become attached to the accompanying shame. I often wonder whether those whose fortunes have been built upon a defiant refusal to be held accountable for their or others' actions and failures to act might naturally cringe or scoff at invocations of God. For them, God is a reminder of laws, promises, and debts better forgotten. But I do not descend from histories of power. I descend from a history of daily miracles by which the soul of a people whom institution upon institution has sought to annihilate yet lives on.

Where does the soul reside? In the heart, the mind? Some believe the soul of a person is tethered to the body by an invisible cord so that it might journey and return. And the soul of a people? I believe it is strongest and most active in the generations of those who claim and conjure it, who nourish it with praise and serious laughter. A people's soul is like a vehicle, conducting the many forward and through, no matter how hard things are, no matter how heavy they get. Daddy Gene accepting the helping hand of his sons, not with sullenness or shame, but grace, pride even in what they're willing to offer. Richmond Brown Sr., born two decades before Emancipation, living in the first year of a new century among children and grandchildren on land that will belong to their people for generations. Emma Brown beside her husband, mother to sixteen, God only knows where some have been taken. Frank Smith, deep in a coal mine. Mama Rose, lifting up the sons America seeks to knock down, saying, *Don't worry, baby. You are bound for great things.* Simon Tricksey Sr. drinking coffee at his daughter's kitchen table, then going to work to coax beauty from somebody else's garden. Even my father, doing his best and surrendering the rest to God. Rather than cynical, the Freed are ever resourceful. We can afford to be no other way, the freedom we've been granted being less than what is promised, less than what we know to be possible. And yet, by the effort of our souls, it becomes ever more.

You who believe yourselves Free, who have perhaps been reading this with a mix of curiosity, skepticism, and pity, what would you do if I were to tell you that we are, all of us—you and me, the Free and the Freed—equally captive in our collective enterprise?

Am I wrong? Is power freedom's prize—a weapon to wield; a currency to hoard; authority to evict, erase, extract? By whose measure are these heroic acts?

Just look at us—the soul of America roils with warring weather. But what might this nation stand to learn from a people whose soul alone has carried them through centuries of storm and war?

I am flying home to California on the day my father will cross the mortal divide. I am rushing through the terminal for an early morning flight.

There is plenty of time to reach my gate, hours before the boarding process begins, but I hurry nonetheless because I don't know when my father will let go. I make haste because I hope there is space between him and the snag in this living fabric where I might wedge myself, and convince him to stay.

I am racing, praying my way to the gate. And I am realizing that the cold damp November California night that took my mother fourteen years ago is only three weeks away, as the calendar proceeds. A decade and a half collapsed by this proximity, once again, to death.

How many times have I caught this same flight before? Once, fumbling to lug a suitcase while pleading into the phone with a man who had chosen another woman over me. Suddenly that old weight returns, the burden of being left behind. My habit, all throughout that once-ago heartbreak, of having to stop and sit down on strangers' stoops, of struggling to rise from bed, of yanking shut the curtains to choke out the sun, because I'd been left and—how could it be anything anywhere but dark?

Walking forward along something like an unending airport corridor. Yes, through an airport while something moves beneath my feet so that even standing still—so that even in a time of fright when I might seek to turn back—I am still heading forward. This is how I have been trained to think of time. But even a foretaste of new grief upends that simple notion.

Grief deepens time, makes every instant thick with layers. The charge of grief is to summon, to collect, to all but resurrect. How else can it be that I am inside those other times and, at the same time, here in the terminal? Surviving the loss of my mother. Surviving the loss of a now unimportant man. Bucking against the departure—dare I accept it?—of my father, who at this instant is both hanging on and racing away. How else can it be that a decade from now, the grief of this very day will intensify my joy, seeing the near-religious way my son leans over a plate of rice. As if my father is there within him studying the grains.

There is the lift of the plane shucking gravity. The lulling bounce and glide of soaring at a great height. Then halfway in with nearly three hours left before landing,

I am jolted awake. No one else stirs. In the darkened cabin, some read, others doze. The crew members busy themselves in the galley.

⸺

Wherever he is now, my father must dwell very near to me. I feel him so often, feeding me memories, nudging me to notice the things that might assist or console me.

Four months after his death, he visits me in a dream. He is clutching a sandwich baggie cinched at the top, full of liquid, an elixir of some sort. Amber, like whiskey, except so bright as to be, in the blue-violet gloaming of the dream, its own source of light. Seeing it, I thirst. It is unbearable how much I need whatever it is that he holds. And as sometimes occurs in dreams, a thought plants itself in my mind, independent of speech. Something passing from him to me, by which I know: what he holds in the bag, what he seeks for me to take, is life.

That is February. In November, my daughter is born.

⸺

In the hospital in Napa, the last place any of us will greet our father in bodily form, he appears to sleep. We circle him in silence. Where is the doctor? The nurses have come and left. It is like one of those awful dreams in which I can't speak, can't ask, can't move from hoping into knowing. *Have I made it in time? When will he stir? If I whisper in his ear will he still hear?* I do not utter and for a long span neither does anyone answer my questions.

Then my brother Conrad arrives. He walks into the room, puts down his bag, and, registering something in our father's bearing, slumps heavily into the force of gravity. Only then does it become clear to me. Only then am I able to accept, too. Our father is gone. The body we have circled, the site of our attention, it isn't any longer him. Only then, giving up hoping, can I ask: *What time did he go?* And I learn it was the moment on the plane, in the dark of the quiet cabin, when I bolted awake as if summoned—bidden—that my father's soul elided with clouds, wind, light.

················

After the sleepless week leading up to our father's funeral—after the arrival of relatives and flowers and even the bouts of laughter at the repast—in the few days before I depart California, my siblings and I sit down to go through our father's effects.

We are expecting something like a scavenger hunt for records and passwords and phone numbers of credit companies. Instead, we find a manila envelope in his bedroom closet onto which he has written: *Kids, you'll need this after I've taken the Great Flight.*

Reading this message in our father's handwriting is,

finally, like watching him go. Not the last breath. Not the soul's struggle to come free of the body. It is him walking to the end of a sentence, the end of a life, and sensing something there worth running toward. It is difficult to capture the enormity of the comfort this affords me.

My father has gone to join my mother and their elders just beyond the rim of the seen. And I am asking language to lead me to the bridge, the brink, the edge of what the great poet Lucille Clifton once called *the lip of our understanding.* Because I understand it is here that the hard work of my generation, the work of living together with others, must take place.

Have I learned anything from that once-ago season? Have I gathered any lesson from the selves that came to my aid as I raced back to California on the day my father would die? All the versions of me, the many moments from my life that made themselves available, like a dutiful procession? The obedient daughter, the jilted lover, even perhaps a future glimmer of the lovestruck mother. I ask because instinct leads me to suspect they'll be necessary again, these selves and others. Not to say goodbye, but to hang on to what must not be permitted to die.

When I was young and both my parents were still alive, our vocabulary for the soul aligned with the teachings of the Bible. This is consistent with Black Christian theology, whereby God is the locus of our attention. To commune or fellowship with another soul was to gather together in a prayer addressed to God. My mother discouraged me from fooling around with ghosts and wayward spirits—not because they were fake, but because she believed demons and false gods were dangerously real. Ouija boards and séances were out of the question. Prayer was all I was permitted, all I needed. As if to affirm this belief, whenever good fortune came my way, she'd exclaim, *Look what prayer can do!*

When my mother passed away, out of respect for the beliefs she held in life, I addressed myself to God any time I yearned for contact with her. But my father—after his passing, he appeared to me everywhere. His wonder at nature seemed to lurch out, as if he were right there beside me, demanding I recognize the bead of rainwater balanced on a leaf, the heron skimming the surface of a pond, the star-swept sky on a clear night. Perhaps it was the effect of my grief, which sought to gather everything to itself like a magnet, but the heaven our faith described—the one into which our souls were meant to ascend, up and away—no longer struck me as adequate for the roving, *sociable* behavior my father's soul appeared to have taken on. It was then that the universe became real to me, no longer a faraway concept, but the actual space where the ceaseless traffic of souls—a traffic in which we ourselves participate—takes place.

My faith was blown open wide, rendered more seamlessly compatible with those other facets of the soul: Soul food. Soul music. Even the rapture and tomfoolery of the once-ago *Soul Train* line. Our laughter. Our bodies dancing. I could—I can—see: we belong to a miraculous, realm-spanning community.

I teach myself to meditate in the summer of 2020. Because I am worried, bothered, hurting. The world—the people in it—seem to be feeling these things, too. All of us, no matter who we are or what we revere, are wounded. Even the people I see as guilty of one thing or another—guilty of harm against the people I love and prize, guilty of harm against me—even they are hurting, too. It is the national condition. How long will the violence, which is the symptom of this condition, persist? How long will we be robbed, day after day, season after season, and no matter who we are, of the fullness of our lives?

And so every day, or quite nearly, as a means of holding myself together, I sit in a black Adirondack chair at the base of an oak tree in my backyard in New Jersey,

taking heart in what seems to be the undeterred industry of birds, foxes, and squirrels.

This house. This soil and grass, these dozen or more
trees we plant thinking we'll never leave. Why should
we? When the movers unpack our belongings, our
sons—babies practically—run up and down the long
hallway. They stand on tiptoes under the kitchen island
ledge, still nowhere near skimming the tops of their
heads. Our daughter sets to work displacing handfuls of
the river rocks someone has been paid to arrange along
the inner perimeter of our yard. We own this place, purchased from the university with the promise to sell it
back should we—why would we ever?—decide to leave.
From the right tilt of the imagination, it is almost as if
we have bought property from family. This house is all
windows and sliding glass. Even inside, a part of you is
outdoors. This oasis for woodchucks and chipmunks,
this gathering ground for councils of robins, cardinals,
and jays. Walk a ways down the common path, back
between the neighbors' houses, and you arrive at a
lake. Deer and rabbits. Common blue violets. Daffodils
in spring. Wild raspberries in summer. When we first
get settled in, one day running errands after school, my
daughter announces, *Cities are noisy. Towns are quiet.*
She emphasizes this last word, as if she does not want
the fact of it to dissipate. One evening we stand rapt,
watching a fox lope past carrying fresh dinner back to

its den. My daughter, born in Brooklyn, raised thus far in playgrounds and subway cars. Now her avatar is a fox. Now she runs barefoot down the path. Now she tromps home announcing she'll make soup from the snaggle of onion grass she clutches in one fist.

Birds, foxes, and squirrels. Even these trees seem to move with certainty through the work of each season. It helps me, seeing that other living things still know what to do, that the terms of their lives remain clear to them, even as so many of the terms that have long governed human life feel suddenly insufficient to the time now at hand.

And so, this practice of sitting—meditating—becomes a form of ceremony. I burn a bundle of white sage or cedar. I seek to slow and deepen my breathing. When I close my eyes, it isn't absence or silence that I find— the goal of some forms of meditation I've read about— but images, figures and symbols in my mind's eye, and words in my mind's ear.

Am I imagining things? I may be. The imagination is the capacity by which we measure what is or what ought to be possible. Is peace possible? A moment of ease in a disastrous year? The imagination is an engine of creation; it supplies the terms of our longing—our wishes, appetites, and needs—by perceiving what is missing, and then exerting the creative effort required to fill that lack. What do I long for? What do I believe myself to lack? One thing driving me to this rite is the desire to no longer be alone. The need to no longer simply call out, but to be answered back, no matter what the message might reveal. And not by the human chorus that is always on, everywhere, singing judgment, indignation, and fear. I have lived a long time tuned to that. I have bolstered it and heeded it. I have added my voice to its ranks. I have, and so have you. Look where it has left us. Singed by rage. Run aground on the shallow banks of our own panicked voices. Queasy from our treacle of virtue, all the empty phrases we've been taught to repeat. All the flimsy notions by which we seek to convince ourselves we're large. All the easy gestures promising to absolve us of wrong. What we click, like, admit to on the depthless expanse of a screen. GIFs, comments, memes. I want, instead, the opposite of this nonsense. I want to know what my father now knows, to see what he has by now seen, to ask finally what living on this side of the mortal divide means. How I long for him—for *him*—to tell me these things.

Once, sitting with my eyes closed and my attention focused within, I envision the silhouette of a standing figure walk forward in profile and kneel, arms outstretched, forehead to the ground. This action plays itself in my mind over and over until finally it occurs to me that this is a suggestion. So, I get up from my chair and do what the figure within my mind's eye does. I walk forward and kneel to the ground, arms outstretched, forehead to grass. The darkness behind my closed eyes changes into a ring of blue sky surrounded by trees. When a glowing green and blue light seems to spread through my body and fill me with peace and thanks, I fight the urge to leap up, open my eyes, run inside, and announce what has just been visited upon me. I stay. I wait. Gradually, the scene shifts. More silhouettes— this time just the heads and shoulders of many figures. A crowd. I cannot make out their features, but they face me, closing gently in. I feel surrounded by goodwill and protection. Nothing material has changed. I am still in my life, still in the very same day full with the same psychic freight. But I am as if compositionally changed. Filled.

What will save us? I have asked, wresting my attention from the news, from the predictable comments, contributions, even the donations I feel compelled to make. From my professed faith in the processes and institutions that seem—though I hope it isn't true—to creak and rattle in ways they never before used to. *What will save us?* I am often asking, broadcasting it out, practically, to whatever might be willing to console or else finally disillusion me. And so I ask it again now, prostrate in obedience to an orthodoxy I never before sought to possess. Until now, because—*What will save us?*

Kneeling in this way, head to earth in my backyard in New Jersey, I hear a voice. By which I mean: a thought, fully formed, plants itself in my mind's ear. It is not sonic but rather telepathic. And resolute. Distinct from the thoughts that usually emanate from me. On my knees with forehead to grass, the voice—the foreign thought—answers my question: *We will save us. But we will not do it alone.*

Another day, outside at the foot of the tree, I hear the invitation, *Come to the mountain within.* As if the work of meditation can be simply attempting to stand still at its peak. Cardinal song seems to undergird the phrase, now a kind of mantra, *Come to the mountain within. Come to the mountain within.* Then other birds, jays in an on-and-on drone, help me to articulate a thought of my own, to recognize the expression of a new intention: *I want to call something forth.* Birdsong carries the thought up so that it hovers in the air around me. It is a small thing to launch a thought into space. But to feel it met and lifted by another living thing? To hear it rise and spread until the whole yard sings it back? I am elated. I ring like a cicada.

What is speaking to me? Is it me? Partly. In writing poetry, I have come to accept that there is a part of me—my unconscious, likely—that knows more than I know, and fears less than I fear, and can say and hear in language things that my everyday self, left to her own devices, might shy away from, not wanting to hear. I believe that a larger version of myself—my soul, maybe—comes to my aid when called. But now, having sat for some time at the foot of that tree, conversing with what- and whomever will greet me, I don't believe my soul is alone.

If my father is there, it is not in the way he has visited me in dreams. Not grounded to the self I once knew, perhaps no longer recognizable, but rather immense, elemental, attached to the full force of his existence. Maybe he brings with him all the selves he's ever been: the five-year-old at his grandfather's forge, the young man on his way to Detroit, the airman, the husband, the provider, the reader, the supplicant, the Hubble hopeful, and others besides.

I think, too, he brings with him a crowd of souls whose lives—not gone but occurring on the other side of that bridge he finally crossed—might help me endure the intractability of the world I know. So much so that, more and more, when I sit down to meditate—when I burn the sage and close my eyes and deepen my breathing—my ceremony extends to include a question: *Is there anyone who might be willing to come forward?*

Some mornings, the only dialogue to ensue is with myself. *Am I really hearing something, or is it just me? Am I making all of this up?* I have come to believe this apprehension is Logic, seeking to dissuade me from devoting my energy to something so improbable. Logic, making me feel foolish, impatient. I wait. I grow tired, humbled. My mind goes off looking for my father, begins to wander the red dirt roads of Sunflower, the orchard rows, the barn stalls. Often enough, I feel the familiar jolt of almost falling asleep. But if I persist with the intention to receive, something is often offered. Patterns of movement and shape. Changing hues—purple, then a deep evening blue that whorls and swirls, circling before disappearing into black. Dark silhouettes against red. Shoulders and heads. Figures arriving a few at a time, standing above me a moment before lowering themselves down to sit or kneel at my height.

How many are we? I ask the familiar assembly, sensing they have appeared to me before, trusting there is less that distinguishes me from them than whatever it is that aligns us as kin. When they answer, I hear their voice as a single thing in my mind's ear: *Many are we.*

Is it possible to transmit the wave of elation and affirmation that rides in on that phrase? I am claimed, accompanied, recognized! It is as if I am being reminded that what I have entered into, and where I now find myself, is a state I have long known. Not the panic, not the isolation, not the despair of the human moment I am living through. Those things are urgent, yes, but they're also, something assures me, temporary. My original state, one they have arrived to remind me of, is here in this vast, steady, patient, abiding *We.* This We that assures, *Your suffering is real. It is not new, nor is it private. It belongs to you just as you belong to something larger than yourself.* This We that, of all the things it might seek to do, is willing to be of use to me. This We that has arrived to remind me that We, together, have long known what I, in this lifetime, believe myself only now to be learning.

Oh, Logic. I can feel you here beside me, puffing yourself up in refusal to corroborate what I am saying. *There's no proof,* you tell me. You want me to retreat to the factual, the concrete. You want me to trust you to be the arbiter of the possible, the credible. But for all the acts and facts to which you will gladly attest—things few will seek to deny—how much else, in your apprehension, do you dismiss? The power of love, faith, even the resilience of hope in the face of so much and so many seeking to annihilate it outright. When I think of these things, when I bear witness to their use in my life and the lives from which mine has sprung—lives that ought not to have been possible, or bearable, or to have borne such fruit—well, Logic, I am inclined to admit that perhaps you are a mere thing, a meager thing. I know there's no escaping you, not fully. But there are spaces where you simply cannot apply, times when I must concern myself with an authority beyond yours.

I am not alone. There are age-old counter-logics by which communities of people have yearned beyond the scope of what logic has authorized them to expect, or hope for.

For centuries, the people from whom I descend have taken part in ring shouts, a cultural practice rooted in praise, song, and the soul-sustaining power of something so unperturbed by logic as to call itself the Holy Ghost.

For centuries, Black people in America—people whose access to the privileges and permissions associated with Freedom has been monitored and, more often than not, policed—have maintained a connection, however removed, to this rite. Maybe the ring has disbanded, but the songs remain. Or maybe the songs are faint, but the *Amen* is near at hand. Maybe there is barely a song left, only an instinctual deference to the once-ago men and women who died insisting we are God's children.

I claim these people and admit their claim upon me.

Their ways have come down through the generations, reverberating as words, whispers, wails, and the rapt silence following laughter or prayer. Their ways—and I believe they, too—are here among us, unseen but gathered, adding heft to our mirth, propping us up in our grief. They are a presence from once ago, active and alive even now with power not yet—perhaps not ever—spent.

I want to call their presence, and what it spans, *Time Ago.* I want to appoint it as a beacon we can yet turn and yearn toward. *Time Ago,* I want to say, is the force that binds the ring into a thing with no beginning and no end.

Gathering in a circle, ring shouters sing, pray, clap, and move together in unison and via call-and-response. Rhythmically, they enter into a shared heartbeat, which some have likened to the effect of the drum in African tradition. Not coincidentally, the rite has direct ties to West African spiritual practice, and it's likely to have offered the enslaved a space where the galvanizing percussive force reminiscent of African drums (drums themselves having been forbidden on plantations) could be replicated via other means.

Amid so many layers of meaning and presence, the focal point of the ring shout is held by what many know reverently as the Negro Spirituals. Call them what you will—they are songs like "Wade in the Water" and "Follow the Drinking Gourd," which offered solace to the spirit of a people enslaved, while also providing coded instructions on how and when to go about escaping to freedom. On its surface, "Wade in the Water" reminds listeners that just as God delivered the Israelites from Egypt, one day He will deliver all His servants to the promised land. And the urgent message encoded in the song's lyrics advises runaways to walk in the riverbanks in order to avoid being tracked by slave catchers and their hounds. Similarly, the lyrics of "Follow the Drinking Gourd" make veiled reference to the Big Dipper, which points to the North Star, the literal lodestar for a runaway fleeing to freedom.

Even for those who may never have endeavored to escape slavery, every song in the spiritual canon offered a hope-fostering reminder that freedom was a possibility available to one's children or loved ones or faraway kin. In the bleakest of circumstances, even that sliver of knowledge must have been a miraculous consolation: *If not me now, then perhaps them soon.*

And so the heart, the hope, the capacity to survive was thrust out from the self in the here and now and forward into an *Us* or a *Them* abiding in *Soon.*

What does it mean to make peace with a thing like *Soon,* to reconcile oneself to what will be withheld perhaps indefinitely?

Soon as in: *One day—*

And *Soon* as a way of admitting: *Perhaps not soon at all—*

Soon as in: *Keep the faith, don't dismay, we can make it—*

Soon in the face of the interminable, the unbearable—

Soon as encouragement against the indomitable—

Soon imparts the force of something other than human and the staying power of something spanning more than a single human lifetime. *Soon* is the longest game. One scaled to soul-time. When a person stands up in church on Sunday and sings—

Soon and very soon,
We are going to see the king
Hallelujah, Hallelujah,
We are going to see the king

—they do so as a way of putting the losses and indignities of the day-to-day into perspective with the scope of the soul.

Soon insists that what is sown, salvaged, and summoned will bloom, keep, and reverberate forward into every future.

Soon is a capacity, a cosmic clock. *Soon* is a way of pledging allegiance to what we are gathered into after the borders of the self and its ego fall away.

I won't lie. There is a sliver of my American imagination that wavers at the thought of self and ego falling away, the individual in our culture having been endowed with godlike sanctity, or so it would seem. But in practice are there not limits? The Black body, the Black ego—have they ever been perceived by America as inviolable? In America, the Black self, standing alone, has been nothing if not vulnerable. On an auction block. In clear view of an assailant's bullet. Even merely within earshot of a whispered taunt or threat. Vulnerable as we are, we who are Black have long known the borders of self and ego to be permeable. And yet, there is respite in this knowledge, for when the ego is hacked down by words and acts, community steps in to soothe and protect.

In 1987, after my father is denied U.S. Department of Defense employment due to his lack of education, just as he begins to slump under the fear that he's exhausted all options, he accepts a job with American Airlines as an aircraft technician. In the last chapter of his career, at age fifty-two, with a son in medical school and a daughter dreaming of college, my father returns to square one. He becomes an airman again.

If there is a part of him that is anything other than relieved—if this job is in any way a blow to his pride (I feel like the spoiled child I must always have been even to wonder such a thing)—it is my mother who consoles him. She teaches him to see himself correctly. He is brilliant, hardworking, and wise. He's provided diligently, lovingly for five children—and look what all they've done. She is proud of him. She feels lucky. She reminds him of something from their early life together: How they saved their honeymoon from the clerk at that Jim Crow hotel. How she'd do it all over again from that day forward, from earlier still. When she says this, the souls of everyone they love are suddenly there in the room with them.

I believe there's something else we summon in our coming together, a source of succor and presence that further attests to what waits in *Soon.* I hear it in between the words in old gospel hymns like "We'll Understand It Better By and By." I hear it in the places where time's shifting nature, bolstered and deepened by grief, peeks through. We are more, then. We are many. We minister forward and back to ourselves across an inexplicable divide. It is evidence of some unnamed law, a clause we have not been taught, but which nevertheless on occasion can be seen to apply:

By and by, when the morning comes,
when the saints of God are gathered home,
we'll tell the story,
how we've overcome,
for we'll understand it better by and by.

We abide in an ever-unfolding *Soon*. We are not over-come. We shall overcome. We will understand it better, *By and by.*

It is August 2020, a late summer morning deep in a difficult year, and I am all but overcome. *Why am I here? What am I supposed to do?* In meditation, I sit, I breathe, I wait. I pass through all the stages of self-consciousness and disbelief, by now so familiar as to assure me I am in the midst of a practiced rite.

And then, with patience, a voice arrives to address me: *We are born, again and again, into every age. We live we die we return. This is our purpose.*

Oh, but the litany of names! Our beautiful Black names! The names of the Freed have become a never-ending dirge, ever-lengthening and always close to mind! I cannot bear to repeat it. I will not accept that our purpose is merely to live, to die. I cannot leave it at that. As if we are simply the raw material of a system with no volition of its own, a machine that, once set to run, must complete its course. There is too much, working too hard, to convince me that my fate as a Black person in America is to be consumed. There are too many, waiting too eagerly, for me to accept this as fact. I push back: *Why does it hurt so much? Why does the world hate us so much?*

Something tender, an audible smile, softens the reply that follows: *Just imagine how God feels.*

I am hearing a woman's voice. A mother's voice. My mind lights up with the joy of claiming kin. *Oh, sweetie,* she is telling me, not with words but with tone, *this is not some pat thing we are talking about. This is Life. It is huge. It is heavy. It is hard for everyone involved. Not even God is let off easily.*

She leans so far from her previous remove as to become visible in my mind's eye. Not as a figure, not as a silhouette, not even as a form so much as a presence. Something pulsing and alive, pale pink and bathed in a liquid white light. Like an organ. Yes. As if we are all birthed through this force, this source.

What I hear next, what I allow myself to receive, is this: *The purpose of our work—the purpose of living itself—is not to be embraced, not even to prevail, but to continue spreading love in whatever way we can. Planting something the earth needs. Seeding the planet so it might proceed.*

Is this another way to understand the work of *Soon*?

Throughout my life, I have heard the spirituals sung in church and played on records certain Sunday afternoons, in the family room in Fairfield, California. I've heard my parents croon and hum and reference them, felt in my chest the swell of recognition when they reach me in the world as if of their own determination. I have accepted them, and likewise the gospel promises of *Soon* and *By and by,* as balm in heavy times. But I have not ever felt them as close to what must be their original source as I do when I witness them in the ring shout for the first time, enacted by a troupe of practitioners in the American South.

I am traveling in coastal Georgia and South Carolina to conduct research for an opera libretto I have been commissioned to write, though beyond the nouns *Black people, land,* and *history,* I am hard-pressed to describe what the work will be about. I am traveling with a composer, several members of the opera's administrative staff, a historian, and two musicologists. Ours is a fact-finding trip. For me, it is also a feeling-finding trip. I am seeking to bump up against the discomfort and unrest—the credible conflict—that will lead me to discover the story I have agreed to tell.

I do not have to look far.

Perhaps because my collaborator and I have signaled a good many times that our story centers upon Black people, land, and history, or for other reasons altogether, we find ourselves as lodgers at what is described as *the oldest plantation in Georgia remaining with its original family.*

The original house is small, Colonial. There are cats

inside, lolling around amid books and dolls and furniture objects that intimate—or are they attempting to *perform*?—the presence of history. But we are sleeping and eating and being greeted in a newer, ample, many-roomed structure that resembles a converted barn. This fact is, for me, a source of minor but perceptible relief.

One of the first things we are told is that our hosts, a mother and daughter who are descendants of this property's *original family,* have set aside thousands of acres of their inherited land for conservation. I don't know whether the slave dwellings have been preserved, whether they are still standing farther away or if they have fallen or been razed. But safe are the oyster mounds and shell circles that bear witness to complex Indigenous societies predating the arrival of British subjects by thousands of years. Welcome are the non-native species—invasive, some have been deemed—refugees of an ever-dwindling global habitat. Surveying the tall marsh grasses and the moss-laden trees, a part of me agrees. A golf course or a gated neighborhood tract here would be a diminishment. There is a plausible heroism to holding such things at bay.

Perhaps, in the context of our visit, there is little point in broaching the various varieties of violence and the inevitable forms of theft making it possible for this family to maintain enduring autonomy over this land. Maybe it is correct that I hold my tongue when our host opens her arms to the morning sun sifted through the boughs of a live oak and asks no one in particular, *What did we do to deserve this?* I tell myself I am here to listen, to gather, to glean. In my head, I steam, fume, roll my eyes. But for the most part, I save my talking for a later time.

On our first night, we are served a traditional eighteenth-century dinner: corn soup, creamed oysters, something with rice. I'm curious but refuse to be impressed. Neither am I delighted to dine with our hosts, whose job, it seems, is to behave as if we are welcome guests. How difficult is such a task? For my part, it is a labor to keep my thoughts from where they wish to go. It is labor to sit beside the elder of our hosts and submit to the rhythm of her voice rather than letting loose the one ranting in my head—the one wondering who would have made and served the food in the history we are being invited to imagine, and where she would have slept, and what specters would have come to her in bed, and what familiar demons she would have risen to with each new dawn. I keep trying to unfurrow my brow, to erase the thoughts nagging me with the commonsense interjection that I have no business being here.

That night in my room at the top of the stairs, the one facing the moon-illumined trees, I brace myself against a collision with the souls of this place, living or otherwise. I pray for deep blank sleep, no dreams. Yet I sit awake in bed imagining a Black woman in a pink dress. She eyes me quizzically.

I don't want to be here, I tell her.

Neither did I, she replies.

I tell her I just want to get through this journey and make it home to my family. It is a fictive encounter. Nothing but my own imagination haunts me.

Nevertheless, she answers. Her answer is a question. *But, girl, aren't you free?*

On the second morning of our stay, we are driven to a town where two-story vacation condos radiate in from the water's edge. While we wait at the ferry landing for the boat chartered to sail us through tidal rivers heavy with oysters and history, I confide to another member of our group that I am bothered to be staying at a plantation. In the commiseration that swells quickly between us, I liberate my face to perform its dance of vexation and disgust. I give voice to the dustup in my head, how the ancestors of our hosts wrung an enduring fortune from the bodies of men, women, and children enslaved on land now protected as an ecological sanctuary. How these same victims of the *peculiar institution* were deprived of autonomy on land now operating as a branch of the nostalgia industry. It feels good to trample the ruse of gentility. But no sooner have I exhaled than I am made to acknowledge the accusation—of incivility? of impropriety?—that flies my way when the plantation daughter locks eyes with mine. I am reminded of certain Sunday school matrons who, with a single swift look, could call the salvation of an entire family, rightly or not, into question.

The historian in our group asks us to do a mental exercise. What must it have felt like, to the enslaved, to live in the shadows and the margins and the silences of white plantation life? How must it have felt to be forced to surrender authority over yourself, your children, the fate of your family? He tells us what we ought to know. That the countless rich facets of the lives of the enslaved are marked, most often, by silence in the historical record. That a true accounting of where we are, and what has happened here, is impossible if we accept such silence as fact. A white man from South Carolina, he relates a story of pushing back, of sitting in his office one day and asking Black women dead now hundreds of years for permission to piece together their stories. He recounts the relief, and the fright, that met him when these women answered back that it was all right with them if he went ahead and tried to tell their stories. Then he directs our attention to the landscape.

It has been here the whole time, inviting our comment: the placid glassy water, muscled moss-slung trees, marsh grass asway in any breeze. This is the South's topography. But as with history, it is possible to see and not to see at the same time. These channels and banks, this labyrinth of waterways broken up by strips of land and vegetation, they aren't happenstance, but rather the remnants of rice fields back-breakingly engineered in the heat of the Georgia swamp by men dragged in chains from their homes in West Africa. Men captured precisely because of their expertise vis-à-vis how rice was—is—cultivated.

At this, our vessel's captain, a reedy, bearded man in his thirties, is surprised: *I thought we didn't use them for rice. I thought we used the Chinese.*

And for an instant, I behold history through his eyes. The capacious *We* which accommodates him. The legion of interchangeable *Them*s, each attached to a unique utility. Later, from the safety of my own privacy, I will take aim at his certainty with the weapon of laughter. It's all I can do to defuse what is otherwise grief. Who knows if I will succeed? What I dwell upon in the moment is that I can't quite pinpoint why this perception—*I thought we used the Chinese*—is preferable to him. Has too much been made of the debt his nation owes my people? Is there more than enough, as he sees it, that will already never be repaid? Has he tallied up the conditions Chinese workers endured during the laying of the transcontinental railroad? The Chinese Exclusion Act? The history of yellowface in Hollywood? Is there room on that ledger for yet another debt?

Out across the water, a paper factory spews its ammonia stench into the air. I can't decide if it hangs over the day like an admission of wrongdoing, or simply as another act of existential disregard. Even so, it is possible to peer up at the broad cloud-swept sky and gaze off toward the green at the far edge of the horizon, with something resembling calm. This veneer of peace and gentility that seeks to invite, abet, and insist upon our forgetting—even this is historically accurate, a reminder of the extraordinary campaign by which a centuries-long crime has been downplayed. Beauty and euphemism are weapons in that campaign. But the arsenal is vast. It is astonishing how quickly the traces of human enterprise can be eradicated. Not coincidentally, human memory follows suit. In this fashion, the guilty and their beneficiaries are absolved.

Back on land, our historian guides us to take note of several unmarked historical sites: a bridge that was at one time the location of one of the region's largest recurring slave auctions. There is only a table and benches there now for passersby who might want to stop and picnic overlooking that particular bend in the river. Many fail to know. To want to know. But doesn't the land know? Don't the trees? Doesn't the water that reaches these inlets from the far seas carry the weight of knowledge, too? And if all know, if all is known, what is it that rankles me so?

It is this: I am worried that, in assenting to the custom of silence and erasure, we also plunder evidence of a persecuted people's miraculous resilience. Bit by bit, we are denied the opportunity not only to ask: *What has happened here?* But to answer back: *We have! We have happened here, and here we remain!*

....

This is the place that is pleasing to the ancestors.

I feel as much even before he says so, or I simply want to feel this way, to trust that I am being welcomed into a place built upon reverence for the lives—the bodies, spirits, and minds—so much else appears to deny.

It is a living museum. Meaning, our hosts, Jim and Pat, a married couple, live here. It is their home, and it is also a cultural center. Talks, tours, classes, parties, even prayer retreats are held here, we are told, as they invite us to enter what feels—from the animals underfoot, to the books and instruments and food and murals and chatter of presence—like a hub of community life. Yes, there are objects on display. Antique photographs. Weathered wood-and-iron tools from the era when the region's *original families* first began to accumulate their great fortunes. Some implements are mounted onto walls. Others from the same period—pickaxes, iron kettles, a cane harvester, and things I'm unsure how to accurately name—remain in use, as if to say, *We are working together with the ancestors; we invoke and acknowledge them.* This, I imagine, is one source of the ancestors' pleasure.

This site, these three acres, once belonged to Jim's grandparents, who descended from the generations enslaved here when it was still an operating rice plantation. The cornerstone of the big white house built by Black hands is still grounded here. It is surrounded by other things similarly bound to *Time Ago* yet anchored also in the here and now. A praise house waits perched on bricks to be restored: What new praise will fill it? A thatched-roof African round house whose form calls out toward home. The original well: the memory of water drawn in from everywhere and drifting back out again. The plantation bell: *Time to work! Time to rest!* All alive with new purpose, and an old story our hosts have made it their work to tell and retell.

I know you, Pat says, looking unhurriedly into the face of our historian. *You're the one who got most of it right.* She stops there, having emphasized the word *most.* She doesn't explain further. She doesn't have to. But she gives him credit for something, and we are all invited to sit, to talk, to eat, to stay the night even, if we wish.

Do I not also register a shimmer of trepidation? As if the wish to trust us and what we have set out to do has won out over an abiding knowledge of how much there is to get wrong, to trample. I cannot blame them. They are guardians of something that has been so frequently handled, and in the handling, so often defaced. But the impulse, their prevailing directive, is to offer, to share, to embrace.

This is, after all, everybody's history.

....

When I return to my room, the woman in the pink dress, a figment my imagination has conjured to fill a lack, is reading a magazine on my bed.

You're back, she says, not bothering to look up. *Where'd they take you today?*

I tell her about Jim and Pat. About the praise house, the cornerstone, the well.

Praise houses used to get hot! I always sat in back next to a window. I wasn't trying to sweat through my bodice.

We laugh. Her legs are crossed at the ankle, and I notice her long feet are ashen and dry.

I retrieve the tube of lotion from my handbag and take a seat on the foot of the bed. I lift her feet to my lap. I warm the lotion in my hands, then work it over the top of an arch, between the toes, under the heel and the foot's leathery ball, before circling the bunion, the knobs of an ankle, the bulb of her calf. I rub with my thumb along the scars and creases of a knee. One coat, then two, as many as it takes. Now the other foot, now back again to the first. It has been centuries since someone has worshipped her. I want her skin to glisten like it did when she was brand-new. I want her to shine like she has only ever belonged to her mother.

On the third morning of our stay in the Low Country, we visit an island where the state has dutifully reconstructed cabins first housing the enslaved, then purchased by those same families after Emancipation. The plantation owners fled during the war, then came back to reclaim part of what they'd temporarily lost. Descendants of the original Black families are said mostly now to have left. The reason cited is a stalled economy. Could nothing have coaxed it to run? Now the economy runs on tourism: vacation rentals, artisanal boats, small-batch rum, organic indigo, iron-wrought mermaids, and handmade cakes of soap. Riding the ferry back to the plantation, I am left to wonder if one outcome is really any different from the other.

That evening, we attend the ring shout. During the twenty- or thirty-minute drive to the performance site, we listen to a recording of the very rite we are on our way to witness. I hear both the strength and fragility of age in the voices and in the simple clapping of hands, the complex conundrum of flesh and spirit, the fleeting and the permanent. The burden I have carried these last few days, the burden of knowledge and silence, lightens. No one speaks. Perhaps, like me, the other passengers allow themselves to weep.

The male performers wear denim coveralls over white collared shirts, wide-brimmed straw hats, and black brogans. The women are dressed in embroidered purple tops and colorful headwraps, and wear white aprons over long indigo skirts. Even before they say anything, their garb makes history visible. Not like the dolls or the tiny rocking chair serving as props in the original plantation house. There is something about the performers' living presence—anchored in our time, but grasping firmly onto something from *Time Ago*—that forms a bridge between where we find ourselves and what—finally—we are being invited to acknowledge.

Their remarks offer narrative framing for the songs and choreography of their gestures, a historical grounding upon which to situate the embodiment of what is, instantly and unmistakably, legible as sacred ritual. They sing, sway, pantomime scenes of toil and escape, speaking back and forth to one another from within the dramatic situation of each of the songs. We have come here hoping to research an opera. And an opera—epic and enduring—is what we are witnessing together this night.

Some among our group of onlookers clap, some hum along. I feel myself lifted from my own cognition of what I am watching and what I understand its cultural significance to be, and into a complex spirit-centered state. I have been sad here. I have been subject to a swirling anger, to constant reminders of my stake in a collective grief. Now I am lifted above the register of mere feeling to a state where my spirit is allowed to interact with the spirits of the performers, and with the spirits of the songs themselves, which remain attached still to those who brought them into being as a means of overcoming the daily excoriations of slavery.

There is a way to listen to these songs as artifacts, to sit outside the ring and ponder or presume to know what leads these people to gather. There is, in other words, a way to process a ring shout as a spectacle, and to come away with an impression that what you are regarding is an act of *anthropological* significance. Such a view is authorized by logic. It pins the living whorl down, makes the viewer—the interpreter—large, when really the whole aim of such a rite is to summon the whirlwind so that it might lift everyone up and never set them down. You should not watch if you, too, don't wish to be handled by such a force, if you don't seek to be delivered from one place—one state—to another.

Another response to the ring shout, if experienced not in parts and pieces but as a whole dark varied sea of love and grief, loss and gain, life, death, and so much in between, is to admit that it is Holy, something it hurts to regard but which also, if regarded properly, heals. For though its first practitioners lived daily with evidence that they were seen as but the fuel of an indomitable machine, the ring fostered assurance of an order larger than slavery to which they were essential. Their power God-given, their work was not merely to endure but to manifest, to remind themselves and the rest of mankind about why all are here. (*Planting something the earth needs. Seeding the planet so it might proceed.*)

The scale of Black hope has never been content with a single person's freedom, or even a single people's freedom. Rather, it is grounded in the wisdom that genuine freedom brings with it the transformation—the true liberation—of all of humankind. It aims to save every *Us*, every *Them*, every *You*. How useful *Soon* becomes in managing such a scale.

See that band all dressed in white?
God's gonna trouble the water.
Looks like a band of the Israelites.
God's gonna trouble the water.

See that band all dressed in red?
God's gonna trouble the water.
Looks like a band that Moses led.
God's gonna trouble the water.

Those figures in the image, the ones dressed in white, in red? They're not an apparition of distant others caged within a faraway past. They are us, now. They are us and every real and present *Them,* now and always. If we can accept the sight of ourselves together, whoever we all may be, then whatever we are working at, whatever we are seeking, we will be working at and seeking together, in this the *By and by.*

I ride back to my temporary room in the plantation reveling at this notion, rapt to imagine an aperture of convergence within our grasp. I don't dream. Neither do I pray. The woman in the pink dress has left. All flights of my imagination are held at bay. But something peopled and powerful is here with me, within me.

I sleep, wake, pack. I have survived my visit to an antebellum labor camp. I have been spared the histrionics of confrontation. I can return home now with a new vocabulary for living—for living together.

But if this is true, tell me, why does a part of me still dread writing these lines? Why am I spilling them out now in an attempt to be rid of the memory? Why am I as if plagued, years later, by the timbre of our hosts' voices still fresh in my ears, this mother and her daughter, descendants of the original plantation family? The older one is dead now, I recently read. Her daughter has surely forgotten how, on the morning of our last day, she snapped at me for arranging my fork atop a plate as she cleared it away: *Stop trying to help me!* The phrase bobs to the surface of my mind even now.

My father talked about his death only once with me before it occurred. It was in his lungs by then. We could hear it drawing near with each breath. *If Mom could do it, I know I can, too,* he said. As if death were a feat we must prepare ourselves, eventually, to complete. And I believe he was right, that with courage we can cross out of what we have long known, and back into what we have, perhaps, always known.

My mother, on the other hand, did not hesitate to acclimate me to the fact that she would one day die. When I was short-tempered as a little girl, she'd tell me that one day she would be gone and what then? When I refused to listen, she'd warn that one day I'd long to ask her the very questions she was just then answering, answers I was too restless to take in. Whom would I ask after she was gone? What would I do then?

When finally her death was in sight, when it had winnowed her strong body into something frail and slack, sometimes she'd make reference to the future none of us could bear to accept, though it was only months, only eventually weeks away. *You should go to graduate school,* she advised me. *You're going to be a writer,* she foretold in 1994, in the last weeks of her life. Of course she was right. All of this on the cusp of the *After* before which my father, siblings, and I cowered. If she was afraid, it didn't show.

Many years after her death, I come across pages written in her familiar script upon which she sought to put into words the reality of God in her life:

God spared my life many times. At an early age I was very ill. The second time, was in 9th grade. We had arrived at school and a few of us were sitting on the bus. Our driver was a high school student and all of a sudden decided to take off, heading off campus. Well, in those days, we did not leave campus until 3:00. We had a strict principal who punished with a wide wooden paddle or a leather belt. As the bus began to move I opened the door and jumped out! When I awakened I was confused. I didn't know where I was. I had my lunch money and kept saying, This is not mine . . . This is not my money. *The third time, a freshman out of college for summer, I went swimming in a creek, slipped and almost drowned.*

Her way of making sense of these experiences, and of the death she was, by then, aware to be near, is to conclude that she was saved for a purpose, that her living mattered, and not solely for herself. There was an order to which she not only belonged but to which her belonging was instrumental.

This is not the message America sends Black people, not in my mother's day and not now. But it aligns with the message of institutions like the Black family, the Black church, like the Black college my mother attended in her youth, institutions that have taken it upon themselves to tell their members we are indispensable, to instill in us a sense of our sacred worth. No matter what or who may seek to violate our persons, this worth remains intact. It is like the soul. God-made. Eternal. Though it be denied, it cannot be seized, sold, or destroyed.

In my mother's case, this message, handed down from generations before, served to foster a difficult tension, a poise whereby the inviolate worth endowing the self must also be honored in another. It is a labor of patience to claim one's worth, to stand straight in the face of presumption or attack, and to resist the urge (it is real!) to strike back. It is an act of saintly restraint to remember, as James Baldwin urges his nephew to remember, that those who presume and those who attack *are your brothers—your lost, younger brothers.* My mother remembered. So did the great souls of her and every generation. Of course, there are outliers, those whose words and actions contradict the sense I am seeking to locate. Nevertheless, this temperance has been a hallmark of Black life in America for centuries.

What about those other voices, the other stories swirling in my head? The ones demanding I go silent, that I *Stop trying to help*? Perhaps the lesson of inviolability is not given to the powerful, but reserved for the oppressed, for the belittled and demeaned. The reason being, there are other lessons the mighty must endeavor to learn.

See that band all dressed in white?
God's gonna trouble the water.
Looks like a band of the Israelites.
God's gonna trouble the water.

See that band all dressed in red?
God's gonna trouble the water.
Looks like a band that Moses led.
God's gonna trouble the water.

Those figures in the image, the ones dressed in white, in red? They are us, now. They are us and every real and present *You,* now and always. If you can accept the sight of it, if you can understand it in the right way, whatever you are working at, whatever you are reaping, you will be working at and reaping together with me, in this *By and by.*

Can you live with that? Can you live with me? Even if it will require you to loosen your grasp upon something to which you have been clinging a long time, tightly?

Can I live with it, with you? Even if it will require me to cede some stance, some sense of the world, which I have been prizing a long time, too?

What if we are being told, by the violence rippling through the world, that our living must not any longer be solely for ourselves? What if my living is an act that must be used to make it possible for you or for her or for them, whomever and wherever they are, to survive? What if the object each of us is undertaking is no longer an individual life, but a collaborative work massive in scale, which finally we must admit has long spanned lives and times? What if our survival, and that of every force alive alongside us, requires that we learn to admit we are bound to something outside of ourselves and outside of the time to which we seem or believe ourselves to belong? Not as a retreat or escape from the experience of difficulty, but as a way of moving past the limits of fear, pain, and ego, and into the fullness of our actual selves—the fullness of actual reality. What if these are the terms of the freedom we in this country so desperately seek?

What might we stand to gain if we were to but adjust our gaze to the scale and the stakes of this other larger undertaking, this colossal enterprise to which each is essential? Not in the hereafter. Not on the other side of the divide between death and life. Perhaps not even in *Soon.* But here, today, where we ache and grieve, and where our best effort is mightily needed. Where we are gathered not merely to enrich ourselves, or to absolve our dead, but for a purpose scaled—what if it might be?—to the soul's stake in eternity. Can we choose it? Can we cross the bridge from here to there?

I struggle to imagine where such a journey might begin, where the cosmic might be broached or bridged. I am frozen trying to solve such an elaborate equation, until something causes me to understand it as the work of paradox: we approach the large and the far by means of the near and the small.

I sit often lately to meditate. But sometimes I shy. I'm not sure why. Today I sat outside in exquisite almost-fall weather waiting to receive whatever might be offered. I apologized to the guides—my familiar We—for only turning to them when my mind is caught up in a frenzy. I acknowledged that it must be difficult even for them to deal constantly with such doubt, need, and anxiety.

A voice answered, *It's like trying to help a drunk*

friend. Someone you love who just doesn't have all their faculties about them. And I laughed. Then I relaxed.

Soon, I felt a jolt, like the kind right before falling asleep. Then, very clearly and in full-color vision, I felt myself to be soaring through clouds, rising above the clouds on a bright sunny day.

I turned my head, eyes closed, to take in what felt like a wide panoramic view. I saw golden light and mist. I had the distinct recollection of the poem "Angel," by Kamilah Aisha Moon—sweet dear Aisha, when she was alive, to us, her wide circle of friends. That moment in the poem where Michael Brown "saw himself / *running into the face of God*" in a dream:

> Weeks before, he called his father at 1 a.m.
> after his vision, voice trembling.
> Dreaming, he tried to remember
> if Heaven was anything like this place—

There was a moment when I thought to look down toward the earth. I saw landmasses and water from the distance of a great height. But I also saw dark haze, parched dirt, red light like sirens or flame. I heard nothing but felt myself within a desperate din. It was frightening. I couldn't help but open my eyes, afraid this was a scene of what might come to pass. Indeed, what has already for a long time now been happening.

I t is 1999, and Diego and I have been living together in California for almost a year, in an apartment on the ground floor of a two-family house in West Oakland. A working-class Black neighborhood. One I too often hear myself scurrying behind with phrases like *—but it's safe,* and *—but it's close to San Francisco.* The gesture is involuntary, like a tic. Its trigger resides in the region of my mind implicated when certain people ask where I grew up, which isn't here, but isn't far off, either. The ones who, when I locate myself and my family in geography, will perform the math that leads from there to class. My life has been riddled with these people. They are endemic to California. They look down from their hills and out across their shore. Their pronouns, even back in the time I'm remembering, are particular: *Mine* and *Ours.* Unwillingly, near daily, I authorize these transactions. I smile, I comply: *—but it's safe. —but it's close to San Francisco.*

Along the sidewalks in our neighborhood, passing

only and always Black people, Diego carries his slight body more rigidly, advertising a heft he does not in fact possess. Does he greet them? Almost. He tightens himself, lifts his chin then dips it back down, nodding, or nearly. Eyes held steadily on the path forward, hands in pockets, feet fast, hurrying past. Preemptive. Not wanting to be slowed down by what they might ask. Sometimes he feels obliged to speak, to reply. *Hey, man,* he complies. *Hey, man,* wielded like a shield.

To him, I am not one of them. We have history. Chemistry. There is still some whiff of pursuit in the air between us. Another thing that distinguishes me, something that sits beside the *amor* we make and profess, is the desire, the insistence, to give. I provide. My depth is a font. What I'd be obliged to do anyway for myself, I do instead for myself and him, *con amor.* And so, for now, our depths mingle, mine tipping to fill his. I for one would like *for now* to last a long time.

If Diego has seen Black people before—and he insists that he has, in his country—it is as if through binoculars. Black tourists peppering the beaches in Cancún. And farther inland, too, shopping or dining or posing for photos along wide colonial avenues. Our faces on TV. Our laughter and tomfoolery in movies. He tells me over and again that his friend Antonio's mother—a woman from the state of Veracruz, a woman he's known since he and Antonio ran around barefoot as children in *la primaria*—he tells me over and again that Antonio's mother is *even as Black as you.* (Always, with Blackness, there are degrees.)

Mere days before we happen to first meet, from my hotel room in Mérida, his city, capital of the Mexican state of Yucatán, I linger on a cable news broadcast originating in an American city. In Maryland? Indiana? I wish I knew. A construction crew has drilled into a gas main in a Black neighborhood, and an explosion has ensued. It is morning there, and here as well. The people in Annapolis or maybe Indianapolis are delayed on their way to work and as they hurry children along to school. Meanwhile, in Mérida, I linger on this broadcast while my sister Jean and our friend Rose, my companions on vacation, rouse themselves with coffee.

The first eyewitness account is delivered by a woman in a sweatshirt and fall-weather flannel. *Did you happen to observe what led up to the blast?* she is asked.

And she answers: *They was digging and digging and digging and digging—and it blew up!*

The rhythm, her bouncy mounting cadence, is fun. It is funny. I laugh. Jean and Rose laugh. And yet I also go to the place where I can't circumvent certain thoughts: *Why did they have to ask* her? *Why did she have to do* that? *What suspicion does she confirm? What darker message does she convey?* It is a lump that returns every so often to my throat, a function of the double consciousness this nation requires Blacks to possess. When will it ever become just a relic, this habit of seeing what the wider, whiter world is made to see as a result of our presence in this—our, their—country?

Next, the camera cuts to a woman with bird bones and big eyes. She doesn't wait to be asked a question. She is already at the climax of her narration, which she punctuates by the raising of her voice, activating of her body, and widening of her eyes. As if each of these things, her voice, her body, her eyes, are instruments to be applied. What she says together with what she does looks like this in my mind's eye:

\\\///
I heard a loud sound go — **BOOM!!!**
///\\\

With her, again, I undergo the same quick cycle of asking, acknowledging, and brushing aside. Then I give in to a form of delight at the spectacle of our—of Black—witnessing. The way a question, to us, is sometimes a form of goading. A way of urging *Do it! Do it!* And how often we comply, gathering it up—the ongoing unceasing—with our bodies, our voices, and giving it back as something we have briefly contained, something bearing our mark. The translation by which the extractions, the excavations, the evictions happening constantly around and to us are birthed out into common space. A shudder, and then: *I saw it! We've seen it! I see it! We see.*

I've told this story through the years to my aunts and cousins, and to my non-white friends, sliding my own body into each young woman's bearing. I've refrained from relating it to the white people I know for the same reasons I knew better than to enact it for my father: because it bears the whiff of minstrelsy. The theatrical Blackness of her cadence. The splendid choreography of her recollection's arrival. All brought nimbly and dangerously to bear upon the answer to the question all are asking, and none will ask.

Meanwhile, on Linden Street, Diego observes our neighbors—Black mothers and grandmothers and young Black fathers shepherding school-aged children through crosswalks; Black couples parked in front of houses, stereos thumping; Black men talking in a group on a lawn on a quiet street (our street is a quiet street); a Black man behind the wheel of a luxury sedan; Black women in hospital scrubs; a Black figure thin as a wire asking for money near the highway overpass; even our landlord, the heavy Black man who lives quietly upstairs—Diego sees them all as the terms of a hypothesis it is his task to elaborate and refine. Every day this hypothesis is being written and revised in his mind. Its every step begins with the phrase *Black people* and proceeds ahead inevitably toward the words *don't* or *always* or *never*.

It's funny how Diego's seeing, like the roving beam of a searchlight—*There's one! Over there, there's another!*—intervenes upon my own. I love him, therefore I seek to intercede, to lay the pavement between him and them with my own wordless conciliation. Because I know how easily they must register the way he heavies himself against the phantom prospect of attack, like a hiker who one day—he is sure of it—will happen upon a bear. And so I attempt to create for him, with my attention and my intention, a buffer. With my smile, with my nod—The Nod I am authorized, by my race, to give and to expect—I demand that the people he fears, people *even as Black as me,* regard him not on his own but always by way of me. Anyway, it is not them I am worried about so much as the vexing effect of Diego's fearful anticipation. The last straw he might one day lay atop what is already a mountain of affronts and presumptions.

Why do I fear for him? Is it because I, too, feel the impatience I project onto them?

We live in a nation that has been trained, and often rewarded, for regarding Black people in this fashion. My mind wants to leap for a moment to 2010—years after my marriage to Diego has ended, years when it might be true to say that the casual regard that skims over the surface of Black lives—a gaze originating from a collective American imagination, an American eye—is beginning to harden into something else. It will be difficult to argue this point for a time. Barack and Michelle Obama in the White House will be reason, initially, to push back against any murmurings of the kind I'm offering. But soon enough, a particular scrutiny, one familiar from an earlier era, will be more difficult to deny.

For me, one iteration of this scrutiny begins in Huntsville, Alabama, when Antoine Dodson, twenty-four and Black, fought off an attacker who had slipped into his sister's bedroom through a second-floor window. In the early morning hours, Kelly Dodson, whose daughter was in the room with her, was awakened by a stranger in her own bed attempting to rape her. In local news footage following the event, Kelly, who is perhaps in shock, sounds tired, resigned, worn down by what seems, from her tone, to be an event that is both frightful and unsurprising. She compacts her story into pieces small enough to sigh out on a few breaths: *I was attacked by some idiot from out here in the projects. He tried to rape me. He tried to pull my clothes off.* This is what initially saddens me about the video, which gained instant viral-level Internet attention and was mixed into rap and R&B-style auto-tune spoofs. How resigned her voice is. How her description of the attack matches the tone of something that could have happened at the office (*some idiot stole my lunch from out the fridge*) or at the mall (*she tried to act like I was going to steal something*). The scale of the grievance can claim only so much space, the victim knows, already knows, has long known. The reporters have only just barely arrived, but for Kelly, *out here,* this story is an old one. Even now, she has reason to doubt anyone is listening.

Then the camera cuts to Kelly's brother Antoine, the hero of the story. He is thin, theatrical. He eats up the camera's eye. Like his sister, he seems exasperated, but this circumstance, in his bearing, is a source of animation, a reason to sound an alarm. He has narrowed his audience down to an insular group—an *us* that is also a *you*—whom he seeks to warn: *Well, obviously we have a rapist here in Lincoln Park. He's climbing in your windows, he's snatching your people up, trying to rape them, so y'all need to hide your kids, hide your wife, and hide your husband, 'cause they're raping everyone out here.* In his telling, too, this threat is not news, in that it did not just begin (*obviously we have*); rather, it is happening, has been happening (*he's snatching . . . trying*). What I hear in Antoine's narration is awareness of an ongoing circumstance that has ossified into fact: *No one is coming to our aid.* Is it grief, in part, that serves to temper Antoine's understanding of time?

Antoine's address shifts to the assailant, whom he speaks to through the camera, stepping in close and punching the air with—is it a rolled-up newspaper, a coupon circular?: *We got your T-shirt, you done left fin-gerprints and all. You are so dumb. You are really dumb, for real. You don't have to come and confess that you did it. We're looking for you. We gonna find you. I'm letting you know now, so you can run and tell that, Homeboy.*

Kelly Dodson has been all but spliced out of the auto-tune remix by a comedy music quartet called the Gregory Brothers; she paces in the background behind Antoine as he "sings." Like a guest artist, she pops in with a brief cameo snipped from her original testimony: *Some idiot from . . . the projects . . . tried to rape me.* If Kelly and Antoine use their news footage to give notice of a problem in their community (Is Blackness a com-munity? Is America a community?), in the remix all of this has been nullified, transmuted into a source of entertainment by the Gregory Brothers, who describe as their aim creating *the maximum amount of happiness for the maximum amount of time* via their spoofs.

The Gregory Brothers' remix links to merch: the MP3 single, the sweatshirt, and, unsettlingly enough, even an LP of the siblings digging down deep to draw up their own gospel-inspired simulacrum of "Go Tell It on the Mountain." Their pastiche is intercut with clips of an anonymous corps de ballet, uniformly white in pink tutus and opaque pink tights. Further in, the video cuts to an orchestra conductor and percussion section. A white church choir (suburban ladies in crimson robes and caught, mouths open, mid-*Ah*) add testimony, of a kind. When Antoine sings, *We're looking for you,* archival footage of what appears to be a white mob spills across the screen. An instant later the mob is called off, redirected, revealed to be a crowd of young men, students possibly, commandeering a car in what might be a Vietnam-era protest against the draft. Two of the video's makers, geeky white boys in suit jackets, pop in and out, punctuating the mix with handclaps and dance moves of their own. I am curious about what they believe themselves to be saying when they lip-sync along with a statement like *He's snatching your people up.*

In response to criticism flooding the network after the original broadcast, reporter Elizabeth Gentle returns to the Dodson home. Antoine, calmer this time and holding his niece, says, *What people fail to realize is, our family, we don't run around crying and acting sad. We just dust our shoulders off and keep on moving.* And yet this story, even in its original framing, reveals how much the world is willing to do the same—to dust off its shoulders and keep on moving, laughing as they go—around sites of violence against Black people. Kelly Dodson, with the camera's help, is herded out of her own story and shuffled into the margin of her brother's. This erasure, eviction, extraction is the bedrock of one story the Gregory Brothers tell, wittingly or not, with their track.

Searching up an early reposting of the original and remixed videos, I come upon comments now years old from viewers who consumed the video as entertainment:

First time I saw this I thought the funny part was the interview and I was giggling at work and then . . . the song went on and I almost fell off of my chair laughing! You guys have made my week GREAT!! :D

And:

The funniest part of the video is when he starts talking really fast and they cut him off. His face he looks like an adorable chipmunk.

Such responses highlight for me how thoroughly the generalized *we* of wider, whiter America has been habituated to positioning a speaker like Antoine Dodson not as a witness to be believed but as a figure to be acted upon—to be giggled at and then, in the remixing, laughed at ROFL-style. As someone to be sped up and cut off, to be reverse-anthropomorphized into a chipmunk, at which point he becomes *adorable.* I feel what is, again, the old scrutiny—one familiar from the age of minstrelsy and racial caricature. I have seen Antoine Dodson's words transcribed like this:

He's climbin' in yo windows
he's snatchin' yo people up
tryna rape 'em so
y'all need to hide yo kids . . .

When I was a child, I watched one or two episodes of the TV program *Amos 'n Andy* with my parents in our California family room. Yet I can't corroborate the memory that reruns of the program would have aired in that place and that time. It is the type of evidence a network might have sought, in the decades since, to scrub. But watching Black actors Spencer Williams, Alvin Childress, and Tim Moore clown like that with their voices, bodies, and eyes, I laughed. My parents laughed. (My father also shook his head.) My mother explained that the program, first televised in the early 1950s, was complicated, that the clowns these men played at being were the clowns white people pretended they believed us to be.

When my parents were children growing up in the 1930s and '40s, white men Freeman Gosden and Charles Correll acted out these Black men's parts on the radio. The audience couldn't see—though I suspect, now, they could hear—that the voices didn't belong to genuine Black men, but rather white actors impersonating them. It was okay to laugh with us laughing at them, my parents attempted to explain. But it hurt to hear these white men, who corked up their voices good and black, laugh back.

In my mind, at the time I'm setting out to remember, Diego is guilty not of prejudice but rather ignorance. I decide it is a side effect of NAFTA flooding his country with the swill of my country. A large part of our conversation, Diego's and mine, has to do with the workings of his ceaseless hypothesis, which I consider it my duty to whittle back. If I can only teach him, I can liberate him from what he ought to know better than to say or think or believe. If only I can teach him, I can absolve myself of guilt for the long shadow my country has cast upon his country. But there is a pebble in the shoe of my mind which has to do with the suspicion that Diego might believe—in his ignorance, and its arrogance—that *he* is the one whose job it is to teach *me*.

In Diego's mind, Americans—real Americans—are white, a condition which authorizes them to collapse any and all of the hierarchies by which he has been trained to distinguish himself. When their pale faces turn to take him in, it ceases to matter, for example, that he is not *indígena* but rather *mestizo;* that his is not a family of *campesinos* or even petty bureaucrats, but rather freewheeling bohemians; that he is not poor, but rather, for the time being, merely broke; that his Lebanese grandfather was handsome, wealthy; that in the hierarchy from which he has come, there are rows and rows of rungs—whole *pueblos* of rungs—beneath his own. Nevertheless, in California, the white gaze scans across him and he is sorted, like the items on a supermarket conveyor. He is Mexican. Robbed of all nuance, of all exception. In the eyes of real Americans, white Americans, Diego is a problem. I am a problem.

Do we believe them?

I meet Diego in the autumn of 1998, during the week of Hurricane Mitch, which chases Jean, Rose, and me inland from our vacation rental on a quiet beach south of Cancún. The drama in the heavens and on the highways makes our meeting feel like an act of fate. For a moment, it threatens to prove our father right for warning, *Be careful down there,* though he is thinking merely of the villains—the *banditos*—in his beloved spaghetti westerns. Lately our father, a recent widower busy with a new courtship, notices little and lets much pass. Our orbits during this time cross less and less.

I wake up one morning, alone in the rental house but for a white woman standing above me. *Who are you?* she asks, though should it not be clear? It is her house, yes, but one she has rented to three Americans—*guests* is what we believe ourselves to be. Why shouldn't I, asleep in one of her beds, be one?

She's let herself in with her key. There's a hurricane a day or two off the coast. *You guys need to leave.*

I squint up at her quizzically. She stands winding the cord of a TV into a neat bow. *I have vouchers for a hotel in Mérida, which is four or five hours away. Or I can refund you the rest of your money and you can change your return flights. I'll be leaving in the morning myself.*

She is clipped and matter-of-fact. She warns that there might be blockades of hitchhikers—service-industry and hotel workers—seeking, like us, to flee to safety. People by whose efforts the vacation rentals and restaurants and hotels of tourists are made to run smoothly. Like the young woman named María who, each morning when she arrives to empty our trash and refresh our towels, removes a torn bra of mine from the bathroom wastebasket and hangs it back on the towel rack. As if that kind of waste makes no sense to her. *Can't it be mended?*

Now this woman, the owner, is telling me to leave before this invisible corpus of workers reaches a mass capable of blocking our way. But it is fear of this woman, not the workers, not the hurricane, that quickens me.

When I look, more than two decades later, at all my journal entries from this time, at my dead-on-arrival and do-not-resuscitate essays, all the means by which I have attempted to narrate this trip and what it leads to, I understand most clearly the heavy weather of my own naïveté. I am, that year, a twenty-six-year-old in a post-graduate writing fellowship, where, in just over a year's time, I've gone from struggling to flailing to mute in an attempt to find my poetic voice—voice being a cease-less distraction, a stand-in for selfhood itself, to a young writer.

Even so, I am lucky. I hold a graduate degree, albeit one of limited practical utility. On top of that, I've con-vinced the admission committee at a Bay Area univer-sity that I merit a sought-after fellowship. *We* loved *your poems,* the director says on our one brief phone call. At this, I press the receiver to my ear. I don't want her voice to slip away, her enthusiasm to be siphoned off or dissipate. I have no reason yet not to believe her. I have no reason yet not to indulge the wish that this woman, a great poet herself, might one day become a mentor—a poetic mother—to me.

I am often looking for a mother during this phase in my life. Once, not yet a semester into my fellowship, this elder poet came close to actually nurturing something in me. After the relentless dissecting and dismembering of a poem I'd submitted (I recall one classmate holding up her copy to show how she had drawn a large X through all but one sole phrase, which she urged me to consider keeping) this woman, the great poet professor, had said,

One day, it's going to be a good poem, which by that time did feel almost like something.

No, it has been difficult for me, a writer twice that young woman's age, to overtake her, to wrest this story from her voice. But I have to see beyond what she chose to see.

That young woman was tamped down by grief. Four years after her mother had died, she was ready to be drawn fully and forcefully back into life. Not just life, which was for her then mostly the dim seminar room on that sun-thwacked campus in the expensive town to which she commuted from across bridges and micro-climates, only to be rendered surly and despondent by the grim reception with which her presence was invari-ably met. (Is this last bit fact, or did it simply feel that way?) Just four years into a lifelong mutable grieving—grief being not a room or a house or a state but a nation, it seems to me as I write—and already she sought to be dragged away back into living. Into the livid and chaotic glow of feeling. As if those things—living and feeling, which seemed to her borderless and wild—were not still regions of the nation she occupied.

This young woman—this once-ago version of me—thinks it is California that cages her. And if I confine my remembering to only just that time, part of me still agrees. California. Do I have to unpack it? I have lived nearly fifty years shorthanding what it is about that place, thereby containing the gall it is even now capable of inciting in me (*Black people don't* or *always* or *never—*).

California is, of course, synecdoche.

·······

Maybe you'll let me get back to the part of this story that right now interests me if I offer you this: I am a guest at a dinner party near Sonoma in the summer of 2022. Our host is rich with old California land, a wealth he was born into, a wealth that permits or requires of him a certain eccentricity. Late one evening, in a grand room full of writers, finally over coffee, he turns his attention to me. He cocks his head, taking me in. Perhaps I am speaking of the two or three things that embolden me to adopt a tone of audible certainty. Or else there is some other facet of my bearing that makes him ask himself, me, anyone: *Who and what is she?*

Where did you grow up? he interrupts. The tilt of his head, the grin in his eyes. I recognize that I am being asked to help him classify me. And, raised to be obedient, I assent.

Really?! is his reply. And then, *Was your dad in the air force?* When I assent again, he asks, *But what high school did you go to?* His demeanor suggests we are nearing to a punch line of some kind. With my compliance, he is homing in on the terms of my defiance, the particular means by which I seem to have been granted a horizon farther off from what ought to have been my natural due.

Once I have answered his questions, I gather an impression from the air into which he settles. It is an impression I have arrived at often in a lifetime of similarly jocular interrogations. My impression is this: He feels worthy of what he has. The big house on the old land near Sonoma. The commandeering mother, the professor father, both deceased now—or perhaps that's merely how my imagination has chosen to frame this portrait of him. Why not? Isn't it clear by now that he is no longer himself but a token of something in which I need him to have been steeped? Do you fault me? Even if I remind you that he has just done the same thing, in his own practiced vocabulary, to me?

Yes, he feels worthy of where he lives and what he has inherited, worthy of what has been expected of him based on these and other things. He has no choice. He has been reminded since birth of his good fortune. Fortune, his forebears tell him, is logical, methodical, deserved. It is the antithesis of mere luck, which befalls you without your having earned it. This man's notion of worth is a vista from which he can regard, ignore, assess, and otherwise scrutinize what and whom he chooses, with relative impunity. Whereas writing this, I am made to grapple with the accusations—of insolence, ingratitude, and worse—that might be leveled upon me by anyone reading these words who, like him, feels worthy, or who seeks to be.

The young woman in the car on the road from Cancún to Mérida—which is to say, me—what is her relation to the notion of worthy? Back in Mexico, she does a conversion many times each day that tells her she has more than she possessed only days before on her rightful side of the border. It is an equation by which she is made to feel almost rich. With so much math, with so much that tilts her way in the exchange, there is an onslaught of choice. She has the power to choose, which feels to her like power. Through eyes of this kind, how much now becomes hers?

Red dirt in mounds—mangroves thick with white birds—the sky opening up into sudden warm rain—the thick, intimate smell of cattle and pigs—a crystalline cenote surrounded by gleaming wet stones—and a man in white briefs who will dive from the greatest height (if you pay him), whose body leaps up, then arcs splendidly out and down. No roadblock. Only ordinary people trying to get home: a young couple, Victoria and Francisco, who ride with her as far as the city's periphery.

All these snapshots—all this topography—has she thought yet to ponder the terms by which she is offered such things to see? I think of her grandfather striding the boulevards of France, for a few scattered moments in 1917 no longer Freed but Free. From what I can tell, the shift is involuntary. Like passing into another gravity. One instant to the next and you are suddenly more. She opens herself to these streets, people, beasts, taking what they offer in return. She is a denizen of the earth. While it lasts, she claims her good fortune, her presumption to worth.

Jean, Rose, and I spend our second night in Mérida at a nightclub that spills over into a house party on the city's periphery. Riding back to our hotel for breakfast, I decide that this final stretch of our vacation will be exactly like Fellini's *La Dolce Vita*. But things don't pick up again until a few nights later, when Mauricio phones to invite us to another party. Jean demurs, but soon Mauricio is making introductions: *Tracy, Diego. Diego, Tracy,* in the throwaway manner that suggests the two of us won't likely have much talking to do. Diego smiles, extends his hand. Every time he says something, it must be scooped up by Mauricio and spooned to me in high school French. And my reply must be sifted back into Spanish before it makes sense to Diego. Neither of us is surprised when Mauricio gets up for a drink and doesn't return.

Diego walks two fingers across the flat plane of his open palm. Soon, we are wending our way through the quiet streets of the *Centro Histórico*. Warm light halos certain houses where young people sit outside talking or lean in doorways kissing, whispering to each other.

After several blocks, we stop at a white house under a bare white bulb where Diego unfastens a padlock, then pushes open a creaking door.

I'm guessing Diego must be young. And what am I? I feel old, young, afraid, eager. In a few days I'll fly home, squeeze back into my known life. All these decades later, I can't remember anything else about that first night other than architecture. The layout of Diego's house, the colors of the rooms. Did we stay long, speaking mostly with our hands? Did I hurry us back to the party, preferring to play things safe? Lost, these details. All I know is that when he asks, I tell him the name of our hotel.

Two nights later, with Jean translating, Diego seems older. He talks about his family, their house where artists and travelers come and go. A house with no rules. After his birth, his parents buried his umbilical cord at the ancient Mayan site of Chichén Itzá as a way of consecrating him to the land; he could leave, but he'd always return. He'd been in Chiapas in 1994 when the *Zapatistas* took over the *zócalo*. As he speaks, he moves his hands slightly at the wrists as if writing in the air in small script. Why do I lean in toward him, then watch hungrily as Jean translates his ideas into English? I've had two margaritas. I can feel them in my legs each time I climb up to the second-story restroom. When I look at myself in the mirror, I'm smiling. What do I think is happening, will happen?

We finish up at the bar and Diego walks us back toward the hotel. Then he falls back a few steps and asks me if I can stay out a little longer to say goodbye.

I want to say things I cannot say on the street, he manages to tell me, and I can't help laughing. But I want to go back to the white house under the bare bulb and let him say whatever it is he claims to want to say.

In California, when Diego is not simply a tourist in a record store, or when he is not lazing on the grass people-watching in parks—if he is, say, waking to dress before sunrise for an elbow-grease job—he feels himself to have been extradited, love notwithstanding, to a nation of excoriations and condescension. A place riddled with arrogant Americans who despise Mexicans, and with Mexicans trained to cloak themselves in a learned silence, or else to lash back at the barbed world with bravado. Mexicans who instinctively mistrust Diego, who claims to have been prepared for none of this.

When he sinks into one of these moods, I fret. Was it not my wanting and doing that brought him to this country? Was it not my doing and wanting that tugged the vocabulary of our relationship toward the terms of dreams and opportunity? I remember it. Though we communicated easily in Spanish by then, it returns to me in pantomime. In his country we loved each other, and so shouldn't we have been given the chance to do the same here, in mine? I'd seen it before. The borders, the documents, the phase—a season or two—where everything is wondrous and new. A country to lose himself in. A place to stretch, test, grow. Freedom of a kind, and for a time. Then cold weather, short days. A mundane phase. Then eventually the pushing through to something solid on the other side. That was one version, the one I preferred. The other was shallower. Something with the whiff of a bribe.

There had been a months-long courtship during which time we were mostly notions to each other. What did he remember of me? What did he choose to see? I remembered his mouth, his shoulders, his wet hair. Him laughing, stepping back. Things he did with his hands. And also, the many glinting objects I could pick up, haggle down, or else let make me feel large for buying outright at asking price. I'd write him letters in the early morning hours after returning from a catering gig. I had to work because my university stipend, $15,000 a year, didn't go far. A few weeks in we were warned that, because we were on fellowships, the university would declare the amount of our waived tuition as a taxable gift, which would result in money due to the IRS. We'd be poorer for what we were given, is what it felt like. Which felt like theft. Never good at money, never having needed to be, I hadn't imagined there would be a cost to what I had considered a reward.

I didn't burden my letters to Diego with money matters. Instead, I described his world back to him through my own greedy eyes. Mexico, I wrote, was most beautiful to me in the places where something had been broken and built back. Because I was building myself back from loss. *Humilde* was a word I learned at that time. Because I needed to feel large. More than in my classes, where I felt so often mute, small (at $15,000 a year, could that have been an accident?), a voice worked its way out in these letters, which I folded quickly, so as not to think better of it, and sent.

What new satisfaction—what guarantee—arose in me when, gently, Diego's letters began to include gentle pleas? There was some difficulty around the matter of his rent back home in Mérida. Twenty-five dollars a month for the house where he lived. An old house, typical to that place. I wandered its rooms in my mind every night, awake in what had been my childhood room at the top of the stairs in my childhood home.

On days off from working and from class, I'd drive to Western Union and wire Diego the money he claimed to need. I'd visit certain delis that sold prepaid calling cards to Mexico, lingering to comb the aisles for *atole* and Nescafé, products that led me farther still from the state in which I was living, closer to the one in which I longed to be.

Was there not some perverse leverage (visible to him? to us? to me?) by which each of these things—Diego and Mexico and my money and me—from the proper tilt of the imagination, rendered both of us momentarily more free?

Free is another word for worthy.

Rave, rave against the dying of the light, says an English literature PhD student in a documentary on 1990s rave culture. I imagine the off-screen director has asked if it might be possible to bring the two parts of this person's self into dialogue with one another: the serious student of literature and the adamant raver. *Talk to me,* I can almost hear the director saying, *about the poetry of the rave.*

Diego and I watch the documentary in our living room in Oakland. The grad student looks old to me, the way a twenty-nine-year-old in my MFA cohort had seemed exotic and decrepit when I was twenty-three. And so, like the speaker of every poem, who on some level is invoking music, image, rhythmic insistence, and the authority of all of Poetry to address, at least in part, the vulnerable self, I wonder if this possibly twenty-eight-year-old man—slight, white, with tousled mouse-brown hair that might belie a retreating hairline—is, in his own way, raging against the dying of something. The rave scene? His own youth? The certainty that he, in however many years' time, will make good on the expectations of academia and family and even the culture his talking head on my TV seeks ever gently to undermine?

The love seat where we sit is a hand-me-down from my mother's living room. Tucked under a tailored white slipcover, it roils with blue velvet paisley. Mid-century, trim, with squared-off corners, it would have been an early acquisition of my newlywed parents. I don't regard it with reverence so much as sheepish deference. I try not to reflect on its history. It sits against a white wall trying to recede out of view, so as not to glare back with the message that I am dragging it down with my living, my underperforming, the vague terms of the goals I've set for myself, goals whose finish line is far away and impossibly vague. Poetry? *Poetry?* When I use this word in conversations with my father, claiming it as the destination toward which my entire education has been aimed, sometimes he merely peers off in the direction of that distance, shakes his head, and returns his attention to other things. *Either she'll figure it out or . . .* I hate to think of where his thought arrives.

This is one reason for my interest in the student on the screen, in his confident embrace of a vital-to-him counterculture, the permission he's been granted or has merely claimed. I wonder what burden he shucks, here on-screen, professing his belief in the purpose and the meaning of these beats and this pill called Ecstasy, a meaning he is led or urged to tug toward the terms of poetry. Where is he now? What is the name of that film? Can I bear to comb through the four or five of its type, knowing that the ceaseless, shifting, permissive, world-rending beat will mount me all of the sudden again, with all it once promised to portend?

Watching the documentary with Diego, something is lost on me. It slips past my notice that it is poetry with which this student seeks to validate rave culture, when rave culture is one means by which I have been seeking to run *from* poetry. Not forever, but at least until I have vanquished enough of the voices that have managed to quash something crucial to my relationship with my own voice. The ones insisting it is too soon to write about my mother's death—there is still too much raw feeling there thwarting the terms of distance and craft. Voices that push back against traces of my parents' Alabama, the time and place in which, I've been told, Mama Rose once threw a pot of scalding water on a dog for killing her favorite chicken—such scenes are illegible (and possibly indefensible) to a general reader. The withholding of praise by which I discern that religion must be excised from my poetic imagination, as in the poem (*One day, it's going to be a good poem*) in which my mother stands frying potatoes on the morning of the Second Coming. Once, I believed poetry was within me, around me, tappable, discernible everywhere. But here in California I am no longer so sure. Poetry, these voices insist, is in the head. The voice is the voice of the intellect. The memory is a learned memory, a mythic memory, the memory emerging from authorized—*general*—history. It is as such unsullied by still-fresh politics. The polemic is not poetry. Race, unless filtered through the absolving layers of mythology, is polemical. Race, as filtered through the purifying layers of mythology, has been done enough already. Nevertheless, there is some promise in me. They'd admitted as much in admitting me. To squander it, however much or little there may be, would be to default on a debt to them and the institution they represent, the institution that almost made it possible for me to live, for two years, within eyeshot of dignity.

I didn't have a lot, but it wasn't nothing. I had a burgundy hand-me-down Chevrolet, the car in which I'd been driven to elementary school and back. I had a black polyurethane trench coat and patent leather sandals on high platform soles. Wearing them, I felt strong, no matter that they clacked cheaply with every step. I'd loll reading in parks some afternoons, or lie on my belly filling the pages in a sketchbook with words. I wrote letters to myself. I wrote letters to the poems I hoped one day to know how to write, the way some women write letters to babies, waiting for them to arrive. I had so many people asking me, urging me to behave—to live—more practically. Somehow, I had the wherewithal to ignore them. I had time to think. My days were filled with it. Time in traffic, on the train, at work at a desk. Long minutes walking from one place to another where little awaited me save more time. Time, sometimes, when my thoughts squeezed themselves out from the task I was performing, or the conversation I was having, and climbed up to a tower in my mind where I could dwell for a time, unreachable.

It was one voice, really, that stifled me. Why do I afford it—her—the harbor of community?

Decades later, I was invited back to that campus. In a large auditorium, before a public that had come to hear me read, the great woman praised me. I was permitted the bewilderment of being celebrated in a place that had once, at best, seemed indifferent to me. The next morning, in one of those same rooms I remembered from all those years ago, rooms into which daylight poured yet still somehow failed to eradicate the feeling of shadows and haze, she reverted to the tone I remember. The one that had once seemed intent upon destroying me, or something in me. Only this time I saw—(did I?)—that it was an attack instigated not by judgment—(can I trust what I am detecting?)—but panic.

....

It's hard to tease out one rave from another. In my mind, they all fit within one tall dark throbbing space peopled with smoke, flesh, and flashing lights. But Diego and I attend our first rave with an acquaintance of mine from work. He looks like a DJ—but is he? I can't remember; I remember his aptitude was information technology. At this point I am the receptionist in a large San Francisco office. The first time I introduce him and Diego, I explain that we work together. A few moments later this friend corrects me: *We work in the same place, but we don't exactly work together, do we?* He has coarse short hair that changes colors frequently. Yellow, green, ink black. One day, at lunch, sitting on the grass in a park near our office, he confides, *So, I'm, like, an octaroon? My grandfather was supposedly half-Black?* This acquaintance has invited us to meet him and his friends at the venue. Once there, he offers us each a pill that will be our on-ramp from the building where the rave is held to the psychic space of the rave itself.

When at first nothing happens, Diego pulls me aside. *How much did you pay for this? How well do you know this* güero? *It's been how long and I still feel nothing. If anything, I feel like I'm going to throw up. What if this stuff isn't nothing? What if it's something that will seriously mess us up?* In his panic, we both become more emphatically aware of feeling like (and of nearly but not quite being) the sole specks of brown in a warehouse full of white (where the *nearly* threatens to eclipse the *not quite*).

Then something happens. I am reminded of the many seismic tremors I have lived through in California, instants—unannounced—when the earth has burbled beneath my feet, as if I am standing on a rug that is just at that moment being given a good shake. Something shifts. And then Diego's wide, open, startled, relieved countenance meets mine. What we each regard is something inside visible reality that neither has ever before seen. Is it real? I want to touch it with my hands, my torso, my face. I want to move through it as if through a colored mist.

Bodies emerge from dark corners. My own body—I can't tell if it is distinct from me, or if it has been bound more tightly to my ability to sense and feel—wanders corridors that open into large rooms pulsing with rhythm. Rhythm is everywhere. I wander out of one rhythm and into another. Am I obeying, or exercising abandon? Everyone is beautiful. This is owing to the pill. Even if you have only ever swallowed it once, however long ago in the past, the particular genius of the DJ will drum up and reconstitute whatever flicker of that once-ago glow waits in your body or your mind to be revived. I learn this at subsequent raves. For now, my mind and body are busy. They seek to help me dissolve into the music, which—I can feel it now—is herding me and everyone else, too, just past the break, just beyond the place where this track merges seamlessly to the next, a juncture I can only discern by looking back, except I can't look back because—look, up ahead—see, there—there, now, is something—

My mind wants to release me. I close my eyes awhile and give myself over to the joy of breathing. I lean against a body or a wall, and slip beyond the borders of my skin. When I look again, a tribe of silhouettes moves toward me, necks and wrists and ankles adorned with Day-Glo collars, bangles, and cuffs. The bass tells me *wait, wait, wait, wait* and I hold still. It is like being moved upon by spirits. And then one kneels down, so I can see she is human, too, and says to me something so simple, so innocent it is almost holy. Gone pride, gone envy, gone deceit, gone the shackles of anger, of memory. Though it is never entirely the case that things and people are what they seem, things and people seem loving and guileless and safe.

I am reluctant to denigrate what feels like a respite from everything barbed and small. I want to believe awhile longer in the possibility of large-scale bodily and spiritual harmony, though I accept it is a trick of the beat, of the bright hypnotic lights, of the pill, of the inevitable comedown that will tumble like silent white balloons released from overhead. Still, I wonder—does everyone here feel similarly freed? Even the Free?

California's Bay Area is diverse. It is so to an even greater degree in the years I'm remembering, at the onset of the dot-com explosion, before smart phones and streaming services, these years when email is still novel, optional, irksome to dial into more than once or twice a day. I don't want to misrepresent these clubs, this scene, as entirely white. Not at a time—then—when so many people of color still live comfortably, affordably in San Francisco, Berkeley, Oakland, San Jose, Fremont, San Rafael, Richmond, and elsewhere nearby. In my season of raves, I glimpse older versions of the B-boys and poppers I'd known in junior high and high school, Black and Asian Pacific Islander kids in updated gear astonishing the throng with updated moves. Watching them is a flood of love never spent. But at raves, these islands of color, of distinct ethnic culture, are just that: islands. I never belong to one save for the times I am drawn to orbit, for a time, a group of strangers whose bodies—wheeling, leaping, pulsing, flowing—defy the limits of common gravity. I am always there amid and beside, often trailing behind the friends of my friend in a group that reads, more than anything else, as white. Most everyone is.

Maybe this is the reason for PLUR—Peace, Love, Unity, Respect—the phrase often used to describe the ethos of chill acceptance prized in these spaces. White acceptance. And aren't reminders like this always in part aspirational, something that can't yet be taken for granted? Like the doors on New York City police cars emblazoned (are they still?) with the words *Courtesy Professionalism Respect.*

One night, in a chill-out room, I lean beside a tall Black man about my age. *What are you doing here?* he asks.

Just resting. Just drinking some water, I say, taking him in through wide worshipful eyes. He's a tennis pro and looks it: godlike and pristine. But I can feel him regarding me sharply. I can feel the rays of scrutiny traveling from him to me.

What are you on? he asks.

I'm not on anything, I know to answer, though it pains me to lie. When he asks who I'm there with, all I can do is gesture off toward I'm not sure where.

Nice friends. Clipped. Dry.

I don't know why he is here, or why he is so adamant in his judgment of a lone Black woman in this scene, but I don't think to inquire. Maybe he's been dragged here on a whim by friends like mine who appear to have abandoned him.

For whatever reason I think to insist, *I trust them.*

Often during this season in my life, I pinch myself with the thought: *If my mother were alive, I could never allow myself to live like this.* This wanton bucking of propriety, as if there is no such thing as the soul, no such place as eternity.

And not without discomfort, I admit: *But I need to be living like this.*

You leave a rave when sobriety descends upon you. And in the years I'm remembering, you wander outside past the hundreds of others in your position, and the scores of men—many of them Black, older, especially thin—who converge on such clubs around closing. There are so many of you, and you are all so gentled, so passive, likely also encumbered by the embarrassment of residual intoxication, that these men can afford to make their transaction into a riddle, a game.

One of them will ask, *What is the greatest nation in the world?* And when none of you answers correctly, the man will answer for you: *A donation!* You'll encounter these men over and again throughout your brief season of raves. The joke, in its familiarity, will eventually become something all of you, together, render a sad thing.

Pulling onto the freeway after what could or should have been our final rave, our headlights land upon a young woman standing beside her car on the shoulder. Her posture is sheepish, like a child who has been caught out in some mischief. A cop's flashlight in her face adds menace to the atmosphere of shame. She is pretty, and white. She is dressed like someone emerging from a different type of club: short red dress, platform heels. Diego cranes his neck to take in more of the scene: her car, also red and somewhat new, askew against the on-ramp barrier. If sobriety is registered in degrees, I am better off than she is. But that isn't saying much. A Black woman and Mexican man, we can't, in our current state, pull over to make sure she is safe. We can't make any mistakes. We drive home slowly, hours before dawn, behind a bread truck that heads, turn for turn for turn, to our off-ramp and then, uncannily, through our very intersection near the overpass in West Oakland.

Here, in Oakland, the Black people on buses and bicycles and escalators, in cars and crosswalks and arguments with the world—all of us restore something to Diego. If he can watch us from the safety of his own imagination, if he can supply in his own vocabulary the terms of what circumscribes us, then he can understand us. To understand something—to regard it even with respect, even to admit its complexity—is nevertheless to announce (to the self? to the world?) that this thing is capable of being held, fathomed, contained. Black people, held, fathomed, contained, afford Diego, if not the luxury of condescension, then a means of momentary leverage. Like the rich man in Sonoma, Diego imagines he has classified us. We prove to him something about the discernment he possesses. After a certain point, even my protestations are accommodated in his flattening, totalizing view. To hold a thing—or to think you do—is to make it smaller than you.

In my mind, there is a convoluted circuitry. I find myself claiming the power lent me by my nationality, my language and education. The assurance of work and, however scant, pay. I gather up all of these things around me as a buffer against the perception (whose perception?) of my race. With Diego—because of what Diego cannot on his own attain here in this place where I have persuaded him to come and in whose terms I am at home—I am allowed to ascend notch by notch and ever slightly the rungs of a familiar hierarchy, at the top of which is the thing that I want: Authority. Better still: Authorial Authority, which to my ear and my mind is the same thing, twice.

Diego and I move to Brooklyn when I get a teaching job that offers to pay but a fraction of what I made as a receptionist. Nevertheless, I am elated, validated. I'll have to temp, bartend, anything to make ends meet. Diego will, too.

We live in a tenement building in Flatbush. Why *tenement* and not *prewar*? Because it is full of dark families, Caribbean mostly, and so the phenomenon applied to contain us requires distinct terminology.

The courtyard of our building isn't accessible to anyone but the super. Mostly, it functions as an acoustical amplifier: it makes us louder to one another. Clotheslines strung from windows dress up our living to resemble a celebration—bleached T-shirts, mended bras whipping like ticker tape in wind. Party voices. Car stereo woofers. Sirens in traffic. A baby's colic. We sound the way Detroit must have sounded to my father.

Around the corner we can buy mangos, coco bread, salt fish, and spiced fruitcake. Living here feels like a form of tourism, for a long time. Tropical, like Mexico. Why not Black, like Alabama, the place of my parents' origin? Because I am in the long process of trying to ascend.

Once, hurrying to the corner store, I drop my wallet. At the register, I reach into my pocket to discover the lack, and retrace my steps in a panic. A few feet from my front door, a man I've seen before, day after day, sometimes drinking from a can in a paper bag, other times asking for change, stops me. He is holding up my wallet the way a plainclothes detective wields a badge.

Do you know why it's important to greet your neighbors? He asks the question twice. The first time I am too surprised, too tongue-tied by immense relief on the heels of immense fright, to reply. How much money is in the wallet? Not much. It is of meager worth. What did the man think when he picked the thing up? Probably that I was just like him.

Thank you, I tell him. *Thank you,* offering what little I can afford. An insult, if he is anything like me. He waves it away.

Greet your neighbors because they look out for you is what he says, walking away. And I do. After that, even to this day, even as the anomaly in places where some neighbors must think I am just passing through, and that I must therefore be verified, commented upon, watched. Even now, I greet them. I do.

After months, it is Diego who realizes the deli a block away across the intersection sells Negra Modelo for $1.25 a can. Not the one with the live blue crabs bound up in twine whose eyes gyroscope around like transistor-operated toys. The one where the woman at the register takes her time with the line of immigrants shipping barrels of T-shirts and household goods and paper plates and dollar-store appliances and medicine and batteries and bright rigid plastic trinkets back home overseas. The woman who knows I'll wait, can tell there is no place I must be, no young family in need of me. She looks at me like I am her pitiful niece who doesn't know better, or knew once but won't remember. Now that Diego has found the other deli, we walk there on Friday cradling loose laundry money, then return home swinging six-packs, or a pack whittled down to four, whatever we can afford.

Soon it has been years. Diego is in school. My world of friends and his world of friends still fail to converge, save for the couple living on the ground floor. He is Colombian. She is from Spain. Our living, which has long taken place in Spanish, now feels bigger. Two of us are writers, two are painters. Or intend to be. With them, in our living room or theirs, we are not American—which is to say not Black, not white, not fixed, not fathomable. There is a part of me that finds all of it luxurious. Out the front door, this changes, of course. Out the front door, around the corner, on the subway platform, I must push back against *Black people always talk to themselves. Black people are always trying to sell things. Black girls have long nails and nice asses.* To shut him up, I call him a *viejo sucio,* a *pendejo,* an *hijueputa.* But I put food on the table. I curl around him at night. I fathom him. He fathoms me.

Once, he tells me a tall tale about a ride to the air-port with a Black livery driver who drove an old ragged Lincoln painted yellow with paint from a can. When we can afford it, Diego spends part of the winter in Mérida, which I tolerate reluctantly because it cuts back on so much complaining. He says the car had a hole in the floor of the back seat. *I'm not kidding! I saw the lines on the road!* This driver's head, Diego insists, bobbed forward, like he was nodding off in the front seat. Again and again the driver would startle himself awake just in time to avoid hitting something—*Como el Señor Magoo,* Diego remembers. *Como el Señor Magoo!*

Six months or even a year later, I call for a car to the airport. It is early on a late-autumn morning, the moon still bright overhead. The car that arrives is an old yel-low Lincoln, painted as if by hand. Inside, in the back seat, cold air pushes up from a hole near my feet. None of this rings a bell until, well on the way to JFK, we veer right just in time to avoid hitting the median. Every few minutes I must yell, *Hey!* to get the driver to look up at the road.

This is how things go in our relationship. I can't always tell what is fiction and what is not. Like the figures in his sketchbooks, lithe nudes, I wonder if he is making things up, or if his life is full of regions and rooms—in Brooklyn, in Mérida—from which I am excluded.

Around the time Diego decides to apply to art school,

I arrange for him to meet a famous painter whose memoir I have been copyediting. The manuscript is epic and rambling. Philosophical, surreal, paranoid, profound. It does not need a copy editor, but something like the hand of God to reach down and impose some interstellar order. To chart a path through it like He once did the Red Sea. But I can't discount it. Much in it strikes me as staggering, sacred.

Diego and I ride the subway to the loft on lower Broadway where the Artist and his wife live. I have been there many times before, to talk about the book. Mostly to listen to him talk, to sit together at the mahogany table smoking cigarettes, sometimes to walk over to one of his immaculate oil paintings—birds and bones and half-human figures—to feel startled, regarded, rebuked.

Diego carries a loaf of warm walnut bread wrapped in a dish towel, and a long, serrated knife. I bear a twelve-dollar bottle of wine. We sit for a time at the table I know, where I have sat long afternoons listening, asking, folding my edits into small phrases that can be delivered quickly and without fuss. Then go on listening. It is in this fashion that I learn about the Artist's childhood. A Catholic Charities orphanage during the war years. The impossible choices his parents were forced to make. The sister he lost there, who got sick and didn't recover. It isn't my story to tell, but I took it in, for a time, sought as I could to offer it care. All my mistakes, my arrogance, my shrinking back from who I was, my fear of sliding down a rung, my seeking to ascend, always to ascend. Tonight, together with Diego and the Artist and the Artist's wife, the target I seek feels far off, farther. I want to be a writer. A poet. I want to climb to the tower at the top of my mind. I want to belong to myself.

Over and again on my visits with him, the Artist has told me the names of the artists he loathes, the schools where his talent was honed, the snubs, the losses, the rivalries, the grief, the hurt, the ego and its needs. Over and again I've scanned the room, a loft, from ceiling to floor, swept my eyes across the windows looking out onto frigid winter white. How the light through frozen day can take on a gruesome gray. Over and again, wondering will such a place, such a life, such a name ever be mine? Will it afford me rest? Over and again, thinking, *Do I know enough about this man to be of help to him?* There is too much my ignorance has kept me from asking, but I have no place else to be, and he pays me.

Tonight, Diego is eager, excitable. He wants desperately to prove something, to prove himself to this man, this master. He wants to earn some terms of praise, codified in prose, so that he, too, might ascend. One day, I know, he dreams of life without the need of me. The thought, which I can smell at times, is frightening. Tonight, he talks manically. He leaps into any pause with questions that aren't questions: *Isn't it—? Shouldn't you—? Aren't they—?*

I can feel the first fissure open up that evening when the Artist takes a look at images of Diego's work. It occurs as if with the creak of shifting ice. *Yes, yes. Larry Poons,* he says. Larry Poons, whom I know he loathes. The portfolio, the sketchbooks, he wants it all cast from sight, cleared away. His reaction reminds me of the afternoon I showed up with lipstick staining my teeth. The sight of it—his arms, his head, his expression let me know it was a terrible affront.

When the artwork is retracted, when the Artist calms, Diego starts in again with his words, his stories, his impressions. The Artist descends from Black Cubans. And Diego has something to assert, to assume, to prove about Cuba and its people, its *negros, mulatos.* He lapses into Spanish at times, and so this is what he calls them: *negros, mulatos,* words freighted albeit differently in Spanish, but we are not in Mexico, not in the Cuba Diego has read about in decades-old books.

There comes a moment—I watched as it first broke the surface, as it began to stir and then roil, no longer repressible. I sat knowing Diego was *tink-tink-tink*ing away at a peace that would not, could never hold.

When it breaks, when the Artist rises to his feet and puts his hands on Diego's slight frame, the Artist's wife—who has been silent and hesitant this whole night, unwilling she seemed at first, but now, I gather, it had all along been something more—shouts, *Let them go! Just let them go!*

And when this happens there is nothing we can do but stand and, finally both mute, go.

This was years ago now. Like a film seen during my youth. But I refuse to give you Diego, as he refused to give himself to me. He was mine the way a teacher could be mine and also someone else's. Could believe in me and also see fit to ready a line of defense against me. Could do this without even meaning to. Could do this and be correct in calling it all—the belief and the defense and the ignorance or happenstance—a form of education.

I turn to Diego here as a figure who helps me move from one room, one phase, one line of sight to another. Always going or coming, emerging from or disappearing into some unlit periphery. If he was ever mine, it was during those months when we were first apart, when I'd write to him after a night of work, then lie awake trailing my wet prints on cool tile back and forth through the rooms of his house. If you are looking for him in any of this, you will only ever find me. That is the final lesson he taught, teaches me.

I want to say this—all of this—is a story about the American Imagination, which envisions itself as a place where all are welcome, a chill white space peopled with minds, bodies, distinct energies.

But plunge beneath the surface, which is bright with reflected light, and you'll find there are hierarchies running fathoms deep. In one, you are an obstacle to be cleared. Or a means of momentary leverage. Or a gauge against which the worthy might measure their privilege. I bob. You drift. We spend ourselves to stay just where we are, near the surface or at some dim depth. Our legs, kicking to keep us afloat, stir up all manner of matter.

We can drift out far. We can rise up to sip air. We can come to believe it is a matter of buoyancy, our settling back eventually at the rung of the familiar, or sifting up ever higher above legions of others.

The sea of us is everywhere. We cover the earth with our surge and our pitch. We cannot see to the bottom, nor past the downward rim of far-off horizon, and we are, all of us—in America, beneath America, full with America, famished for what America has promised—I, we, they, you—all are treading the same water.

I do not want to pull you—or be pulled by you— under.

Is there a shore, do you wonder? Where we can rest, do you reckon?

The smell of children in a house. Clean diapers and wipes, their sorbet scents. The soft leather of new little shoes. Wood and glue. Play-Doh ground into a rug. The sleep-and-spittle whiff of a blanket, a stuffed dog. Scratch and sniff. Stiff cardboard picture books—my daughter, Naomi, gnawed through so many, it began to appear as though they had been sold that way, with the bite taken out. What did my children consume, anyway, except milk and fruit, root vegetables, crackers, applesauce, and sometimes chicken diced into cubes? The first time Naomi tasted cake we were at a café. After the initial bite, she wolfed the rest quickly, handily, and then began to demand, *More tate! More tate!* At first her father and I laughed, but our laughter tipped her into rage, which we remediated with more cake. *More tate.* The smell of certain bakeries is, to me, the smell of children in a house. Because of the cakes we baked—coffee, banana, pound. And also, the cafés I'd escape to for reprieve from the fact that my body, my mind, my precious time—none of these were any longer solely mine.

In the time I'm remembering, years ago now, my children were no longer infants but still quite young, and the arc of my days, as I sometimes allowed myself to see, was to take great joy in waking, feeding, and dressing them, and then handing them over to the preschool or the sitter or what- and whomever I could trust to just take them away. At which point I'd go to campus and teach. Or sit at my desk overlooking the yard and write. Or ride a train into New York for lunch. Sometimes I would get back into bed with a book. Then I'd welcome them back home again late in the day, momentarily filled with the self they would set back instantly on nibbling away.

Remembering this time is remembering a time when I so desperately loved myself that I longed to have her back, wept sometimes thinking of where she had gone. In her place, of course, was me. Bending over a pot. Stooping to rake Legos from under a bed. Sitting in a restaurant across from another adult, keeping a conversation going, while also in my head wondering where she was, when I had lost her, and whether or how she—myself—and I might reunite.

As if there was no guarantee that I'd discover, for some new reason, how to love the me she'd left behind.

The emblem of her absence for a long time was my

waist. She had taken my waist with her when she left. I covered myself in fabric, hid what I had allowed to collect around her lack. A big new girth mossing over the want of the woman, or more rightly the girl, whom I grieved. The one whose youth was spent laughing, running late, chasing intangible things: language, love, harbor from heartache.

In the time I'm remembering, when my children were no longer infants but still quite young, the arc of each of my days, as I'd jokingly sometimes say, was: *Coffee, coffee, coffee, coffee, wine, wine, wine, wine.* Which is a way of admitting: in the time I'm remembering, and for reasons I am seeking only now to recall, my living had become an attempt at forgetting. Then, I did not ask—though I am asking now, or seeking to ask—what, and upon whose insistence, I was so adamant to forget.

⸻

Our twin sons are born into the world eight weeks premature. They will not be released from the neonatal intensive care unit for two and a half weeks. During their stay, a Florida jury acquits neighborhood vigilante George Zimmerman of second-degree murder for shooting Trayvon Martin, an unarmed seventeen-year-old child. A Black child in a black hoodie. He could have been my brothers decades ago, or my father as a young man wandering Detroit. Blood or not, history instructs me to claim Trayvon Martin as kin. My postpartum heart herds him in.

The news of the decision does not come as a great surprise. Not because it is correct, but because America has had centuries to perfect the discounting of Black lives. This jury, like others, has swept an age-old suspicion and an age-old doubt into a mound and heaped it onto their scale. America's streets and schools and cafés and boutiques are filled with doubt's debris, which tips the scale on occasions like these.

In photos from his unspent childhood, Trayvon Martin's beautiful face beams toward the camera. In one image, he stands in a red Hollister T-shirt, arms loose at his sides, held safely in a familiar gaze. In another, he's at aviation camp, standing in profile, looking up from a page of text—a diagram, perhaps, of an object in flight. As a mother, I believe I can decipher some of the baby that lingers still visibly in him, something vulnerable that has not yet been pulled taut. He smiles, teeth parted. Or else he has been caught on the cusp of speech.

The theft of this young life, the needless and groundless but nevertheless familiar loss, adds yet more heft to the understanding that my own tiny boys are born fighting for their lives.

The whole time I was married to my first husband, Diego, I felt like a child sleeping over at a friend's. A night turned to a weekend to a week. Years passed and still no adults arrived to break up the party. Eventually it became clear I was the adult, and I dragged myself away.

I have read narratives of near-death experience in which people who suffer traumatic accidents briefly leave their bodies and travel to other realms of existence. Some describe a multiverse of scenarios: paradises, libraries of knowledge, places of purpose, schools of learning, liminal spaces where the traumatized and beleaguered find temporary rest, and on and on. Others, for whatever reason, are offered visions of darker, denser dimensions. Most return with the certainty that there are realms upon realms, versions beyond versions, each correlating to the individual soul's level of development and need.

There is a subgenre of near-death experience that involves visitations to nightmarish places. *Why are these people here?* the visitor asks of a guide familiar with the place. *What have they done?* Invariably the answer boils down to a form of choice; they were convinced in life that they would end up in hell, and it is the energy of their conviction that created just such a place. After the initial terror, the visitor observes that the hell is unenclosed. Nothing and no one stands guard. There is an exit, a clear means of egress. *Why don't they leave?* the visitor asks again. *They will,* is the answer. *When they realize the choice is theirs to make.*

I live messily for two years after my divorce, then I realize that something other than suffering is available to me. That's how, or rather why, I meet my husband. In the moment of our first kiss, as if in affirmation of what we can hope to reach and share together, the song playing on my stereo breaks into the musical equivalent of the heavens opening.

Years into the future, when Naomi is nearing three, my husband and I arrange to spend a day and an evening in one of Manhattan's old storied hotels. We are still living in Brooklyn. Our nanny will pick up Naomi from preschool, like usual. They will go to our daughter's favorite park in Brooklyn Heights, then walk home for dinner, bath, books, bed.

I don't remember why we've decided not to spend the night. Does it seem more luxurious this way? More scandalous? I think, now, we must want to make an occasion of slowing down together. No computers. No tending to the tasks and chores from an unrelenting semester. A romantic getaway hidden within an ordinary day.

When we get to the room, a serious feeling overtakes me. It is as if an invisible presence has followed us there to demand our attention. Does he feel it, my husband?

The way it vibrates here beside us? He cannot, but he entreats me to describe it.

I think it is my father. Both my parents. They've come to ask—no, to present me with a choice. An undertaking. I don't sound like myself to myself, but my husband draws me close. He dries the tears, which are not a sign of sorrow or fright but revelation. I relate to him what I understand. I am receiving this message. There is something I am supposed to do. It may not be easy—I don't know how it will work, how we will manage, but I am getting the sense that—I'm getting the sense that we're meant to have another baby.

I'm nervous. There has been such a perfect balance to our lives lately. It's not effortless, but it is, in a way, easy. Our one child. The small apartment we own, the one whose study is now a child's nursery. Our big-enough car. The dog and cat. Walking to Smith Street for lunch. Grading papers next to one another in a café. Nothing has been too much. Everything has been enough, more than enough. I haven't lost myself to the juggle, as I feared that I would. Neither of us has. Is my husband willing to potentially upend this perfect balance with me, for me?

I understand now how much more terrified we ought to have been by the stakes we were asking to engage. Naomi's birth had made us aware of our own mortality; it was suddenly imperative that we survive, if only in order to ensure the thriving of this amazing child-soul. It hurt to be away from her. It pained us to see her cry. It was terrible to imagine the day she might push us away, craving her own space. Oh, and the world. What were we to do about the state of the world she'd been born into? The water, the trees, the blight of hatred, indifference, and greed. And yet, in the span of a few hours one afternoon, we were agreeing, though we didn't realize it at the time, not to double this responsibility, but to multiply it by *three*.

When my husband answers yes, that he is willing to try for another child with me, I'm reminded of the moment of our first kiss. Again we are capped by a new enormity.

Atticus arrives first. I wake up to a puddle in the bed. Sheets, blankets, everything wet. No labor cramps, no quickening, but my body has woken itself with this bout of something like weeping.

After the birth, the baby is shown to me for just a moment. I am allowed to hold him briefly to my chest. Like a tiny comet. The scrawny wriggling legs. Warm vernix still slicking his skin. But there is some mention of his breathing, his lungs too young. Quickly he is lifted away.

Sterling is more hesitant. He has yet to descend. My

doctor reaches in. I watch at first as if he is at work in an architecture that is not me. His arm disappears up, up—I had no idea my womb was so tall—to puncture the sac. Has it really been two days of admitting and trying to forestall and then finally accepting the inevitability, and then the necessity, of this too-early delivery? I am ready and I am not ready. For months I've been lurching toward the sight of them, toward the dream of their faces and what they bear. Did one of them feel the same? They could have stayed where they were, but they are here, squinting, hands fisted tight, shoulders raised, legs pedaling against the sudden air, the delivery room light.

But it is too soon. Again, the doctor questions the lungs, their viability. It falls to my husband to race after the nurse as the second new son is ushered away.

⋯⋯⋯

Coffee. Coffee. Coffee. Wine. Wine. Wine.

Because I was cleft. Three lives in four years had been cleaved from mine. Is there a cartoon where a character—a cat or a dog, maybe—runs smack into a saw's whirring blade and is split down the middle? And keeps running, for a time not realizing or not believing he has been cleft? Until finally the two halves fall down? And then get up to continue running, only this time away from each other?

....

The first time I see the boys again they are in the NICU, tubed through the nose and down the throat, slung with wires and tethered to monitors: blood pressure, pulse, O_2 saturation levels, and I can't remember what else. The whole room hisses and beeps.

What have I done? What has being born of me done to them? I weep. I feel at first as though I ought to leave them alone, to let their tired bodies sleep. Haven't I done enough?

It is the nurse who urges touch—and then—

a slow quiet unfurling of the gaze, and something traveling through the skin from across ages to arrive at this life, this life, these lives heavy with intent, they have set out and they have made it, each little vessel is warm, it hums, it sends something toward me, into me, back to where it has dwelled but the beginning is further off still, lifetimes and ages, strange to me yet known somehow, too, the breath, each little racing heart, each tiny pale finger curled around mine, they are mine but they are more, lifetimes more, it's so clear isn't it, that they've known, they know, they are tired from this knowledge, the distance they've traveled, the intent. Let it pulse into me, let them give what they've come

to deliver, let them take what will feed, form, fill
them, I could sit here all day—is it day?—holding
them, dipping my face down toward these faces
wholly theirs and who else is there with them, too? I
am searching these faces, these tiny hands, the warm
scent lifting off each downy head, who else is here,
what have you brought, who sent, who sends you and
what can I do, what can I do but hold, but breathe,
but love, that is what I am here for, why I ache,
what I will do, I will love, love you, I am so afraid so
afraid but fear is nothing beside what you have come
here to do and I will help you I will serve that wish I
love you I will I have always I do.

Identical twins are one egg that divides. No telling what or who it is that decides. Each baby is born cleft from and cleaving to the other. Ever since they could speak, my boys have called each other by the same name: *Brother.*

Naomi, their sister, is older and therefore, to them, Other. Formidable. They regard her with awe. Do they realize she is also a child? I wonder.

Photos of older "graduates" from the NICU line the walls at check-in, kids whose healthy faces and broad smiles are a daily consolation. There is even an eight-by-ten of a husky teenager in a high school commencement cap and gown. My husband and I claim the strength, the thriving of these children for our own sons. The smiling faces that walk us back from fear, intervene upon the daily jag of tears. But we can't let down our guard. We refuse to, because right here in the waiting room where the TV stays on with the volume turned down, here with us in our coming and going, there is also often another face, which the camera cuts to again and again throughout the trial. He is beaming toward some earlier camera's lens. Or he is peering out from under the drape of a sweatshirt's cowl.

The nurses seem to understand this, too. They are Black women and Filipinas, quiet, gentle, steady as bedrock (one in the delivery room had even been named Nurse Rock). They keep the TV tuned to the Zimmerman trial. They remain vigilant in their care. Every life, they profess with their actions, is a matter of many lives. Parents whose daughter fits at first into the father's palm. A new mother so young it seems she doesn't know to fear. All are graced by the saints of this place, who are tireless, who whisper without inviting despair, who teach us to lift, hold, and handle our babies as if they will be our babies forever. They tell us to go home, to sleep, to rest, to recover for the joy and labor ahead.

It is a Black hospital in what was once a Black neighborhood. The white mothers who live here give birth elsewhere. So I don't feel gawked at as my breasts struggle to make milk. So there is no question as to why I cry in the waiting room eyeing the trial.

I feel terrible, still, that this is what my sons first saw. Their mother, in hospital garb, standing above the plexiglass incubators, peering in with such hope, such hunger, and then curling into herself in tears. What must they have taken that to mean?

If my mother were there in that instant, she would have shown me how to claim my children, how to muster the confidence a mother must show. How many times had I studied her hand fanned out upon some other woman's baby's back, the firm and gentle way she'd pat, not from the elbow but the wrist, to coax a burp? If my father were there, he'd have put his arm around mine as I cradled one, then the other. He'd have said, *I'll rock them when they're bigger,* extending a lone finger for a tiny hand to grasp.

When Atticus and Sterling are just barely three, they squat down to fill their plastic ferryboats with bathwater, then stand back up to dump the contents onto the bathroom floor. They know they should stop. I have asked/told/begged/demanded them to stop. First gently, sweetly, then with increasing clarity, then full-on distraught. The message is clear. Still, it's *squat, submerge, splat.* I indulge more than I ought. When will we be far enough from the conditions of their birth—the fraught, breathless *how* and the terrible asphyxiating *when*—for their lives to no longer be a held-breath affair?

········

When it comes time to talk to Naomi about Alton Sterling and Philando Castile, when she seems old enough (she is all of seven), by that time there are also Eric Garner, Michael Brown, Walter Scott, and Tamir Rice. Emmett Till, Amadou Diallo, and Rodney King are there with me, too, when I say what I have put off saying for what seems like long enough.

I take small halting steps, second-guessing myself at every turn:

Most police are good—(Really? Are they?)—*but lately there have been situations*—(Not lately: here in America this happens every day)—*where some officers make mistakes*—(Like when you're angry at your brother, and you think about hitting him, and then you walk up to him and hit him very deliberately and very hard as a way of fulfilling that deep-seated urge, and it's only when I threaten to punish you that you say, "I didn't mean it, it was a mistake")—*and end up hurting people with Black skin*—(Make it real)—*like Mommy's skin.*—(Yes, this thing can touch even us if we are not careful to remain . . . to remain what? Lucky?)—*Many Black people have been shot by the police*—(Say it)—*Shot and killed.*

How do I tell her without killing something in her that it is an old vista, this line of sight across which shots are fired and bodies—Black and living bodies, bodies beautiful and intact—are commanded to fall?

I remember my mother first showing me this fact, by which I mean telling me. We were alone together, as we often were, when she told me about the care that I must take, and the people who might fail to exercise care toward me. However much she whispered, however gently she transferred this information, what I recall is the feeling of a hand gripping my chin, craning my line of sight toward that from which I struggled to turn. Nobody touched me, you understand. It was my own mother sitting beside me, speaking softly, patiently, padding each word with love's freight. But the site of that memory is forever sore. There was, of course, no other way.

Naomi doesn't ask questions. She grabs my hand and meets my eyes with a look of panicked sympathy.

Oh, Mommy— is all she says.

But her brothers. What would I say? They are still

eating out of shallow bowls. Food cut up into neat cubes. How could I tell them their breathing fills me with terror? The fact that it could be punctured, snuffed out, drained away.

<hr>

When the children are asleep, I rinse the dishes and load them in the racks. The bass beat of a campus party has traveled across the lake, though wind and distance have rendered it faint. Our students are surely awake. Our colleagues, in houses up and down the block, might hear what we hear and remember what it was like to be young. My husband washes the skillet with a stiff brush. I clear the linens from the table and jog them to the laundry room down the hall. My husband wipes wine rings from the counter. Outside: wind-jostled trees, a distant train. I lock the doors. My husband snuffs out the lights. We push the world away. We are a couple in love. Night clings to our living like a glove.

<hr>

A cold wind blows down the rest of the leaves, hounding them across the lawn. The dog eats through a box of teabags left on the counter. In the grocery dairy aisle, Atticus answers the question *What's your name?* for the first time without prompting.

Sterling answers the question, too; he says, *Atticus.*

Four aisles later, both boys melt down at a display of Goldfish crackers. *Melt down* makes it sound like something it isn't. It isn't a quiet deflation. It isn't what I resign myself to feeling every so often: a heavy hollow in the chest, the heaping on of what feels like lack. In their melting down, today, yesterday, tomorrow, my sons flare into hysterical need. They rage. They flood the aisle with tears. Their bodies stand up and hurl themselves back down. They are precisely what I have always imagined the weeping and gnashing of teeth to resemble. At this stage in their acquaintance with the imperfect world, they melt down several times a day.

In the silence after, I feel floodlit by strangers' judgment, and by my own shame at the way our living insists upon being seen. I am not imagining things; people stop to watch. A mother I recognize from the elementary school asks if there is anything she can do. In circumstances like these, whenever another woman asks me this question—especially if she is white and more or less a stranger—what my ears hear is, *What do you think you're doing bringing this chaos here?* She is usually calm. Exemplary in her slender life, a life with clean confines and a wide margin for error. Cars stop for her. She pedals her children around in a low contraption trailing behind her bike. And they survive. Often, her children stand watching, too. White and mute, their silence affirmation that our commotion is—that we are—an affront.

Their scrutiny silently hustles us along, renders us itinerant, demands we must be on our way. Where? Where do they insist we are going? How will we know when we arrive?

I gather up my sons and keep pushing, pushing our cart.

I am a Black woman married to a white man.

The happy white families cycling past our house on weekend mornings, the ones trailing each other in descending size order, laughing at some giddy words the father has tossed back toward the dutiful queue— when they cross my path, my whole life wants to hide. Even if I know those families, even if I wave, smiling, rattling off their names, the sight of them is a reminder that something about my family refuses to blend in. Naomi races ahead. Her brothers shout to her to wait up. We gobble up the sidewalk, like a needle on a seismograph. One boy will insist that his father mitigate some rift. The other will cry: high held notes trembling out like a soprano's, plump tears leaping from his cheeks. Each is a fountain of feeling. A font of emotion and need. One needs to be hoisted onto his father's shoulders. The other must be appeased with a joke or a treat. And there goes our daughter, tugging us in an uncharted direction, demanding that we follow—which sets her brothers off. The weeping. The gnashing of teeth. To step out of our house is to play roulette with a thousand urgencies. Chief, I believe, is the need to be seen; next is the need to be heard. We are always out of bounds. I am always made to feel, by our drama, and the strangers at attention, that we are transgressing a proscribed border.

What feeling does the sight of these orderly white families incite in my husband? Does he notice with what authority they claim the road, and how the road can be seen to oblige? Does he notice the youngest there wobbling behind on the smallest, the most gestural of bikes, and understand without a doubt that nothing will befall him—no missed light, no car horn, no rain clouds, no stern crossing guard, no divot in the pavement nor sprung leak of any kind? Beyond a doubt, beyond dispute, everything will make sure he survives.

And if these thoughts occur to my husband, as they occur to me, do they cause his conscience to cloud over, angry at himself for begrudging some deserving child the certainty that he will live out his childhood in safety? The certainty that everything in our neighborhood, our nation, our history has been laid out in such a way to deliver that child to wherever he may seek to go.

Sometimes at night I ask my white husband to see things for a minute through the eyes of his Black wife. To hold our children in his mind and admit that something—some specter or ghost—has been let loose to circle them, to sniff and bellow. Some apparition trained to follow children like ours wherever they might go. And he knows. He knows.

For years now I have watched him, born Free, cradle his children's freedom: different (he knows, he knows) from what's been allotted to him. It is like an infant. He rocks it in his arms, rounding his back, curling his shoulders in, protecting it from cold, sheltering it against wind and other forces waiting to infringe. He leans down to whisper in its ear. There's nothing he hasn't agreed to take from himself and give to them. If the world will let him.

The situation requires vigilance. Some other parent has done a lax job, or no job at all, and that's what has gotten us into a fix in the first place. I tease out another few nits from Naomi's curls. I am almost gratified seeing them there in the tines of the tiny metal comb, knowing that with each pass I am being a good mother and putting a problem to bed. I spend the day poring over all three children's heads, washing linens, bagging up stuffed toys.

I do a fresh load of sheets, which I briefly consider ironing. I am at first wary of a spray bottle meant for the upholstery, but in the end, I use it, just as in the end, I go ahead and use the scathing shampoo on myself.

I regard my children, silent before a movie, relieved of the burden of their infestation. The two little ones in T-shirts and diapers stand bobbing gently on the cushions of the couch. Unobserved, I let my eyes scan the perfect dome of my daughter's brow, her thoughtful mouth, her gaze fixed in exquisite contemplation of a cartoon puppy. Watching them, a rare thought dips into range. Never mind the hours I won't sleep, the words I won't write. Never mind my slack belly, the extra cushion ampling my thighs. Never mind how my ideas these days are like the rabbits grazing our yard at dusk: get too close and they vanish soundlessly into the brush. No matter what, a good thing, a beautiful something, has befallen me.

Funny, but what I most pined for, when motherhood for me was still new, were all the ways I'd once sundered myself, all the ways I'd once managed, even without understanding it, to give myself away. To give myself away to what? To poetry. To men for whom I rendered my body a totem. To languages in which I was foreign. To love and hurt. To dancing. To lying on a couch by a window overlooking the street. To fools suffered. To trust surrendered. To error. To laughter tinged with fear.

....

When I was a young woman still married to my first husband, I spent a summer in a remote pueblo by the sea. One afternoon, I rode to a farther-off shore with three señoras. One of them brought along her pubescent son, who sat the whole way there listening to our chitchat with his hands in his lap like a reticent priest.

The beach where they took me had tables outside a snack shack. Otherwise, it was sun-pummeled and desolate. Sea urchin shells spiked the wet expanse and were made to tumble up and then back as the tide withdrew. It was a sad-happy place that reminded me of the final scene of *La Dolce Vita,* where Mastroianni is dragged back by the gears of his own life after a moment where it seems, briefly, that something else might be possible. Back then, I often imagined being dragged back by the gears of my own life. It was a fantasy to envision that something beyond my own life might one day intervene, momentarily claiming me.

When I meet my true husband, the father of my children, I am overtaken by the understanding that my own life, my intended life, has arrived to pick me up by the scruff, to carry me gently in its teeth.

The señora who had arranged the outing walked to the shack and returned with an orange Fanta and four beers. Sitting in the sun, where the sand had been packed tight by the tide, I felt barricaded by something welcome, surefooted, feminine.

The señora with the boy told him to drink his *refresco* and go collect her some nice shells. When he went, another confided that she was neither happy nor unhappy, but once she had been the mistress of a wealthy man. It was love like a bonfire. When she gave birth to a daughter, he built the girl and the woman their own house—nothing fancy, but *bien cómoda*. When he died, the house naturally passed to the man's rightful wife. The woman grieved. Grief was her one luxury. It sustained her a long time and when finally it was spent, she married a man as reliable as a little coal oven that burns steadily on. She no longer needed to be consumed by love. The four of us sat sipping our drinks, toeing the sand.

I used to have a tiny-tiny waist, said a different señora. *I used to have a long braid that danced down to my hips like a cobra.*

Someone sang a little ditty. One of the ditties everyone on that seaside knew a lifetime ago:

Won't you give me what I want?
You won't miss it when it's gone.

Won't you give me what I want?
You'll hardly miss it when it's gone.
That bit there, from the knees up
And from the waist down.

It's true! the three of them repeated, tickled. *Isn't it true?*

I lost their names quickly. Their faces vanished from my mind. But at different times in the decades since, I have remembered these women. Usually when their living has brushed hands with mine.

⸻

Sometimes what I miss is the feeling of being broken apart that followed delivering my children. Body torn, vacant, depleted. The deep physical bereavement that was the understory, for a time, to the central narrative of expectancy and joy. Understory, because the site of this feeling gets very quickly buried under other things, just as the piles of clothes and books and blankets and all the signs of new life overtake a home with children. In retrospect, it is the easiest recovery of all, one the body knows to do all on its own. These other lessons, setbacks, and wounds run deep, and help in tending them is slow.

I have seen great cats whose bellies, though empty, swing low from having carried litter after litter of cubs.

And I think the whole spirit of a person who has had children is like that. Huge, torqued, visible, heavy still with the weight of what it once held.

The great cat hunts. Sometimes at rest on the plain, she will raise a mighty claw to a foe, will rise on hind legs and demonstrate the intention to kill if she must. Often enough, though, she will merely flick her tail, stalking off. Sometimes of course she must run.

I have left my children at home and emptied my breasts of milk in order to witness a company of dancers onstage in a Brooklyn theater. Their effort resembles delight. Water leaps up from their feet. Water arcs in beads from the tips of their hair. Water flies wide like the radius of desire. Not stopping their dance, they speak or shout or sing—*I'm young! I'm young!* A chorus of them. Their bodies, like bright flags, wave out from a distant territory.

Youth. I remember it. It was a peopled place. There was a dark path, a jostled door, something tapping, scratching, then kicking the thing wide. Or else it began in the knees as liquid heat and traveled up, up. Every appetite swiftly appeased. This is what I tell myself I remember. This is what I tell myself I grieve.

My grief grows most emphatic when there is just one woman dancing alone onstage.

The house is quiet. It's after eleven. It takes a moment to realize where I am. My daughter is splayed on her belly. Her arms and legs are arranged as if she fell asleep climbing a ladder.

The room is full of things that have spanned her whole short life. A self-portrait from the year she was four. Uno and checkers and Sorry and Trouble. Lincoln Logs spilled out from the barrel. Binoculars. A jump rope and whistle. Lego houses, a Lego spaceship and jail. Construction paper piled atop books aslant on shelves. Three wilted balloons. A striped sleeve lisping from the mouth of a drawer. A real hairbrush on a dollhouse living room floor.

I want to stay here with my nose in her hair and repay to her what I hurried to take back when her brothers first pitched in me. When I drew myself away from her like a thief.

I don't have to do what you say, she once said.

And I answered, *Yes you do. I'm your mother.*

And she said back to me, *No, I'm your mother.*

And somehow it was her word that stood.

It hurts now not being able to run back to that first passion between us. Her body small against my chest. Her mouth rooting after the milk whenever she wanted, and the peace—no, really it was the thrill—of being able to effortlessly oblige. Waking up to the huge wet darks of her eyes.

It was a life, a whole long life lived fast. The cloudy blue black of that first winter's sky holding us and pushing everything else back.

I swelled, stretched, tore, sagged, shrank, (sagged), slept less, grazed standing up. I'd stop what I was doing all of a sudden to gaze wistfully at a youthful stranger move as if swimming through daylight. I went to bed and woke up early, like an old lady. I didn't want to, but there was so much to do I had no choice. Awake early anyway, I put in more time. I paid ransom to recover my original body. Running miles at the gym, I fought myself back to what it was I remembered being. Then I had twins and it happened again. My students started to look like my children. My knees made strange creaking sounds, like a historic house. None of the old tricks women pass among ourselves would work. If they worked, it was only temporary. I accepted entropy. I was no longer thirty, no longer forty. It was only upon bumping up against my reflection—it appeared startled, like a ghost, but also tired, dim, puffy, gray—that I realized I'd been holding out hope of being thirty again, forty again someday.

I remember my mom dieting in the 1970s and '80s. Iceberg lettuce, tuna, and paprika-dusted cottage cheese. I remember going with her to a gym that had a motorized belt you slung around your middle and hips. When turned on, it jostled you quickly back and forth like a paint can at a hardware store. I remember cans of meal replacement powder endorsed by comedian and activist Dick Gregory, which we'd mix with pineapple juice and stand drinking by the kitchen counter, gazing wistfully in at a mental vision of ourselves, only thin. I remember the lilac dress with embroidered trim she had me try on when I was in college and perfectly thin, and how the zipper at the waist pinched my skin. *I wore this after I had had three children,* my mother would say. There was pride in her voice, but also the glint of a wish long ago let go. I remember all of this and think, *Okay, maybe I, too, can let it go.*

And yet—and so—I sip, drink, slake. I host parties any old night and it doesn't matter who comes. I sit in a chair and drink and eat and listen and laugh and imagine drifting out over a dark lake toward the lush far bank where music plays. I want to be there, to live there. A peopled place.

I want to love myself the way I had, or thought I had, before.

That. That is what the alcohol was for. An indulgence, a tenderness, something I told myself I—poor beleaguered mother me—deserved.

This is one explanation for the *connoisseur*. For words like *terroir*. It is terror of being pounded flat by duty, hacked past wanting, hauled far from the pleasure of the self—which by this time is not any longer the visible self, but a remembered self, buried layers deep.

And so: sip, drink, slake. The vintage is costly and you are therefore rare. You pay. You tip. You luxuriate (as if this might teach the world how to receive you, how to demonstrate the proper care). You pass around the bottle, eager to share. When it is spent, you signal for more. You care about small things. Finitudes. Is it leather you taste? How is it that you recognize the taste of leather? Unless this wine is a type of bit pulled snug over your tongue.

My husband and I are pressured to withdraw our young sons from a private nursery school because of their classroom behavior—behavior that will soon (but not yet, not in the moment I'm remembering) lead us into community with other families living with autism. Soon (but not yet, not in the time I'm remembering) this setback will be revealed as a blessing. But for now (in the now I'm remembering) I feel hurt. Because my sons are observed for two short days, and rejected as problematic, as unteachable. Because the situation has been handled with what feels like brusque disregard. Because the situation has called their worth into question, and my only form of contestation is to love my sons and press on. I struggle to understand how much of the director's dismissal of their potential has to do with race. The pain I feel on the morning of this decision activates the reserve of pain amassed over the course of my whole life anytime I am preemptively classified, anytime I am judged as threatening or unworthy of bother because of my race. Some small part of the concern I ought rightfully to reserve for my sons is displaced by the anger and hurt hovering around my own untended wounds.

That night, after work, I muddle an orange peel with sugar and add ice, bourbon, a splash of soda. A lone sour cherry is lifted from its syrup. The fragrant bitter warmth restores the boundaries barring any single anger, grief, or regret from aligning forces with any other.

When my mother struggled in any way, her strategy was—she prayed. She whispered, bowed her head, and drew something around her that even in near-silence grew louder than anything else in the room. Her sitting on one end of the couch in the afternoon while I read or watched TV became a center of gravity so profound I sometimes had to get up and leave. Not because she was seeking to be seen, but because the current that quickened and ran through her touched me.

But when my father came home on Fridays, he put ice cubes in a glass and poured three fingers of scotch. He sat down in a chair and for a short time disappeared.

I think about him and I think about her. No one would blink, then or now, at what he did. But her sitting there, the force of her praying, would have been something I hid.

What wants us to disappear?

I drank before I became a mother, didn't I? I had a long life with wine, often starting when the sun was bright, sometimes talking with a friend over a dragged-out lunch, but also often enough at home at my desk, or sitting by the window looking out.

Yes. But I drank more concertedly, with greater fervency, as if to not drink was a form of suffering, only after I became a mother.

I drank because drinking afforded me the tiniest window of time within which I might be justified in resenting my children for needing me.

I drank because drinking was an acceptable form of self-pity.

I drank because loving my children made everything about me larger. And I was told, and dutifully believed, that I should aspire to be dainty, petite, small.

I drank. Because my ego deemed it so.

I drank. Because the vocabulary of alcohol made all of this seem like what it was not.

I drank. Because *all of this,* which I would now call *alcoholism,* was, when I was drinking, made to seem adventurous, sexy, fun.

The alcoholism I hid in the vocabulary designed for this very purpose rejiggered my understanding of what it was that I grieved.

It told me that joy was comprised chiefly of pleasure.

It told me that power was a commendable aim. Even for only a short time, and for power's sake alone.

But it wasn't even power.

⸺

That feeling after a night of drinking, the fear of what you've likely said or done. The copper ringing in your ear, the leaden head that wants to stay burrowed in bed. The blaring relief of being finally assured that whatever stupid thing you did or merely thought—it was nothing, everything is fine, nothing need change.

I'm reminded of how we know better about any number of things, but keep doing them anyway, because they are easy or, in the moment, advantageous. Knowing better but acting as if we don't is a pact we renew over and again from context to context. One day we'll make things better, we'll suck it up and put in the work. But not until we've wrung all we can out of this habitual manner making things worse.

Before I could name, claim, or accept my sons' autism—to be the mother it insisted I become—I told myself it was something I could run from, that they'd mellow with age, that I need only heed the voices assuring me (often enough, over wine) that my sons were wonderful, brilliant, perfect as they were. As if it needed to be one or the other. As if learning to mirror at home the support they were receiving in school was a burden I could delay and delay until maybe one day their neurodivergence would simply go away. Because it was easier, I thought, to sit on my stool at my kitchen bar (it was an island, technically, but I knew why I was there) and indulge a farce.

In the first dream about my drinking, I am standing at a microphone addressing an audience. Try as I might, I can't help slurring my words. My remarks are riddled with nonsense. People I know in real life sit in the audience. After the presentation is over, something unspoken prevents them from making eye contact with me.

The second dream about my drinking begins on the

morning of the day my reputation is instantly and irreversibly ruined. I can't for the life of me figure out what I have done, and nobody will tell me. The dream is permeated by the clear sense that whatever has befallen me is my own fault.

Still, I kept drinking. I began to suspect there was a question I needed to ask myself: *Isn't it time to give this up?* I lived for a while working up the courage to ask, denying it was a question to which I already knew the answer. Standing alone in the kitchen one night, sipping a glass of wine while my young children bathed themselves, the question drifted again into frame, and I looked away in shame.

Walking lately in Harvard Square, I catch sight of a paper notice taped to a historic marker sign:

> *The City of Cambridge acknowledges that this historic marker excludes the history of Indigenous people in this place. A new sign is being made to correct this harmful omission.*

I first notice it walking back to my car. And something leaps up inside of me, an unknown alacrity. *This is correct,* it says. But it says more. This acknowledgment—this admission—stirs up a shame that is not mine alone but that claims me. This notice announces an intent to help lift some small portion of that shame away.

The pact of consenting to something that serves only a few, and accepting it as if it serves all, as if it is the only truth—*knowing better but acting as if we don't*—we do this every day, without thinking, without acknowledging the cost, or wanting to.

Thirty years ago, I would have walked by this historic marker or another like it on my way to a party or rushing from lunch to class. I would have noticed, or not, that it sought to instill in me the belief that the Puritan English had built this place, and that proof of this fact was their names on every building and body of water and street. Reading, I would have accepted such a narrative as truth, not thinking about whom it sought to erase, not asking whom it made small.

But it made me small. Even if my name had been Winthrop or Mather or Standish, such a narrative would have held me, too, in a place far from the fact of what I'd done, or failed to do.

What is sobriety if not accountability, facing plainly what has or has not been done?

Can I tell you a story about what happens every night in bars and clubs and at parties where drunken decisions are made? And as I tell it, will you agree to direct your gaze out farther, past the characters my words conjure, past the bar where you imagine they drink, past even the place where you sit now, reading? Farther and farther still, until what you see is no longer a pair of friends on a specific occasion, but the body—the common history—of a nation?

One night, two friends might sit drinking together until things haze over and one friend says a thing or the other friend does a thing or both together make a choice they know in their rightful minds they ought not to. Harm ensues. Someone is scorned or handled or stolen from. And the one friend there beside the other, consenting in silence, is caught somehow, too, in the shame of that harm. Both go home. Each sleeps it off, then wakes to a vague knowing, acknowledged the next day with a shrug, a choking up the pair covers with hiccoughs of laughter. It is a pact. It binds them to one another. It is heavy. Together they slump to support it. If one puts it down, the weight of it will fall to the other. So they shoulder it, they soldier on. Over time between them there are many more such nights. Eventually, the whole fabric of their friendship grows knotted with compromise . . .

Do you see it? Can you make it out? The borders and treaties, the acts and pacts, the decisions, deflections, and denials? The growing body of history? The integrity of a nation? And how essential sobriety ought to be to such an enterprise?

....

In my particular case, there is an intervention.

It is a Sunday in August, and years ago now. I am sitting at the picnic table in our yard in New Jersey when it occurs to me how nice it would be to be sitting here with a glass of ice melting into a perfectly prepared old-fashioned. How the first sip would promise so much. A reason to close my eyes and open them again slowly, as if I have been tipped back into water and lifted gently up, baptized, unburdened of responsibility. That moment when it is impossible to hear anything—the voice of conscience, reason, duty, scrutiny, the starved soul pleading for attention—but the white noise of abandon. A slow wash of warmth down the shoulders and spine, and down through the column of the throat. A momentary lightening. How whatever weight or freight waits off past the horizon is neutralized in that first nip. Yes, yes, it will continue to wait, but for the time being it will cease to pace back and forth, visible across the distance of dwindling time.

But—something is wrong. The taste is flat, like bonfire ash. An affront. So the drink is tossed. And made again. But, again the second time, the outcome is the same.

I am angry, as if a joke is being played. But by whom? I try, instead, a glass of white wine, which will be cool, clean on the tongue. A lighter radiance than bourbon, but eventually the same effect will come on.

But again. I can't even swallow this time. I lean over the sink and spit, at which point I admit the question— so patient it has been these long years, circling back around gently at times, imploring me to understand what I have long understood without wanting to: *Isn't it time to give this up?*

Yes, I answer. *Yes,* as this habit I have loved—this need to which I've cleaved for most of my adult life—is hauled away. I thought I would feel robbed of something, bereaved. But I am relieved. I am eased of what I have been, perhaps since the beginning, afraid to call a burden.

⸺

Be it personal or collective, sobriety is accountability. Facing plainly what must, or must not any longer, be done.

When I think back now to why I drank, and what my drinking helped me to ignore or deny, what comes to mind are much more recent exchanges. Ones demanding that I allow my appetite to indulge, to escape, and to receive be outweighed by the will to do what parents and elders are obliged—are privileged—to do: provide. Not only for my own children, but for a generation of other people's children:

The student who wrote, in 2020, to say he was terrified by the ambulances admitting his neighbors to the COVID ward, from which not all would return. What he meant, I believe, is that to be Black in his city, and this nation, is to be prevented from forgetting that death knows your name. An ambulance, a police van, a square of sidewalk in the light of day, all might reveal themselves to be conveyances of death, if you look like him, like his neighbors, like me.

And the student petitioning that same spring for return to campus in order to flee the house and the town where their gender expression put them in danger. What they meant, I believe, is that there are people, some of whom we love and who profess concern for us, whose scrutiny hustles us into hiding, labels us a threat, punishes us and others like us who fail to see the world—to see ourselves—their way.

Most emphatically, my mind returns to the handful of students who mustered the courage to address a gathering of faculty (all those aging faces in the Zoom screen, by turns moved, indifferent, perturbed), who risked retaliation in order to tell us the ways we were failing. And how we might change. My mind returns to the outrage of some few colleagues who made it their work to double down defensively, to reinforce and wield their amassed authority. Because they were Free. And also, too, because those students, though wise, though courageous, though correct, were merely Freed.

But freedom isn't a thing to be held or hoarded; its purpose is to be passed forward, given away. Freedom is an impossibility in places where the most one is encouraged to seek and guard jealously is power, permission, authority. Freedom is held captive in places like these.

How quickly everything seems changed, once you realize to what extent everything must change.

Leaving Princeton—the house we love, the life we've shaped—is my husband's idea. He is the first to realize the choice is ours to make.

On Easter Monday, a thirty-year-old pine uproots itself in heavy wind and collapses across our driveway, narrowly missing our house, most of our other trees, and our two cars. It falls onto the only place where it is safe to fall. It falls in the opposite direction in which it had long been listing. It falls directly onto the spot where, an hour earlier, my car had anomalously been parked. Onto the spot where our children sometimes ride their bikes in circles. It lops in half the small tree our daughter has rigged into a treehouse. It wallops the patch of driveway where our boys sometimes haul each other in a red wagon. After it falls, we stand watching from the front windows, shocked, retroactively panicked. It is 2020, and we are at home in quarantine. There is no place else we are likely to be. Two other tall trees thrash in continuing wind. Who knows whether or when something will topple them?

Later, watching the crew remove the fallen tree (and the other two that also threatened to throw themselves down like grief-stricken widows), I remember how much I love my life. How grateful—no, how lucky—I am for the soul-enlarging struggle afforded me by my children. My sons' melting down in the grocery store aisle, and how visible—how vulnerable—it renders me. The complicated hurt of that preschool expulsion. Those weeks in the NICU, with the Florida jury's verdict seeking to overshadow Trayvon's smile, his arms loose at his sides, body open and unguarded so close to the beginning of his life. The heaven smell of my daughter curled against my chest, and the pang of being made to stand up and walk away from that vast sweet world we two alone made. And more. There is always more. All the ways my children—who hold me back from losing myself to comfort and the vanity of authority, the very things alcohol once urged me to guard as my life's chief currency—all the ways they and the other people's children entrusted briefly to my care continue to free me. All the ways they allow me to fortify my own free-dom, bounded though it is, by passing it to them.

The earth-pounding thud of that tree when it fell felt, from the back of the house, like a faraway catastro-phe. Like across town, somebody else's life had been pounded flat.

But it was my life, and what had befallen it was not catastrophe.

The generations-spanning family tree I have begun to assemble resembles the map of a railway system, with stations spreading east, west, south. The northern territory is least charted, north on this map being correlated to the past. But I'd like to take that seeming end of the line as a leaping-off point, an invitation to look up and gather kin from among the living who surround me, the way my mother used to claim the elderly in our community, strangers she'd cook for, residents of convalescent homes she'd take me with her to visit. Then, I took this kind of outreach as evidence of the Christian godliness she strove to embody. Today, I realize my mother must have been piecing together a map of her own, mending the loss of grandparents and elder kin, filling in a constellation that would continue to assure her we reach back far.

My father always greeted older Black men, even those barely a few years his senior, with cordial reverence: *Hello, sir. Thank you, sir.* I used to think it meant he saw himself as a perpetually young man. Now I understand that he was acknowledging, there between them, the history which rendered them heroes, survivors, veterans of any number of our nation's named and unnamed wars. The lesson of this is only now reaching me: that the archive includes our very persons: uncatalogued, uncollected, living, moving, distinguishable at times only to each other.

Often as I've sat writing this book, seeking to move forward into the past by way of words, I've asked the train of souls to whom I'm bound—whether or not I've located them by name—to nudge or even guide me as I write. I hope you will believe me when I say that at these times the air has been thick with them—charged with welcome presence, assurance. Communion across the mortal divide is as easy as asking, as trusting. I believe it is something with which we have been endowed, a tool for our use, a reminder of the soul's responsibility and its continuance. Sometimes I imagine that an older, larger part of my own soul has come to my aid when called. Logic won't be of use in corroborating such an intuition, but the wish adds new terms to the scope of what I ultimately seek: hope.

What will save us? We will save us. We must. It is the work into which we are born. And I trust that we will not do it alone.

I'm trying to figure out how to say goodbye to Sunflower, I tell my uncle Richmond on the phone. I feel tears welling up, as if all this time spent thinking and yearning toward the kin once anchored to that place has planted a part of me there, too. In returning my attention to the present, I feel as though I'm coming of age, leaving home, setting off on my own. I can't bear to turn my back on Mama Rose, to leave her in Sunflower, where in 1971 she will pass away. It pains me to imagine parting ways with Daddy Gene in his dark suit and biscuit-toe shoes. Though I would have been only a toddler at the

ROSETTA AND EUGENE SMITH, SUNFLOWER, ALABAMA,
DATE UNKNOWN

time, I really do believe I remember my father waking quietly in the dark to travel to his own father's funeral in the winter of 1975. I wish I could go now, too, and pay my respects. I wish I could sit beside my own sweet father and cry.

I miss them, my uncle tells me, thinking of my father and their youngest brother, Harvey. *I miss those boys.* I discern the distance in his voice, the years and miles across which he is carried by his own remembering. For him and for me, I decide that none is bound to say goodbye to what abides here with us, in us.

I hear my father in my uncle, the gentle velvet in his voice. I hear him in Atticus already, too, just as one day my children will recognize me in the voice of an aunt or cousin or child. Evidence of the mystery by which we have always been—and will always be—bound. Affirmation that all the family names, all the familiar faces, are here beside me on the couch on a late morning in winter, consoling me in their own real way for the many forms of loss and continuance we are meant to help one another carry.

Mama Rose was born in Sunflower in May 1898 to Fannie Turner and James Sigmund Brown. My father, remembering the great man from his childhood, pronounced the name to me clearly and with pride, though distant cousins say he was called Jim and Sigger and Sig. But he was *Daddy* to Mama Rose. She would have lingered in his blacksmith shop as a child, just as her son, my father, had done. She would have been a little girl then, in cotton gingham or flour sack prints, at home in that space with the heavy anvil and white-hot tongs where bright sparks leapt up like stars. With the hammer's music repeating, repeating in the shop and out from the shop and forward and back through the distance we call time.

We repeat. Our voices, our features, our names. The turn of a foot. The way the heel of a hand cradles a piece of bread. My uncle gives me my father, just as my father carried his mother forward to me. She softened something in his throat, made his voice theirs, something they shared. What I believe echoes, too, is their courage. Their faith. Their will to be of use without regard to recognition or praise. More lives than we can count. More names than we may ever come to know. Essential still to freedom's enterprise.

Let me talk to Jeannie, our great-uncle Theodore used to say when he called. Our mother's father's brother, he lived to be 101 and remembered every detail in the life of his family. He outlived so many of his kin—*my people,* he called them—but offered them to us in stories. When he was five, his father would put him on a gentle nut-brown mare and tell her to take young Theodore to his grandparents' farm. Then he'd pat her on the haunch and the two would mosey down the long dirt road, round a few bends, and trot up the drive to the house where the old couple waited for them.

Put Jeannie on the phone, Uncle Theodore used to say. *She sounds the most like your mother.*

One way we persist is through one another.

By we, I mean us all. The circle of family.

And because so much of what means family has, for the Freed, been excised, cut short and erased, I seek here to reach beyond blood, beyond kin, to conjure the *We* that might harbor every soul made to feel not looked after but watched. Not wanted but Wanted. Those for whom call-and-response is not merely a form, not solely a rite, but the vehicle for a necessary message, the one embedded in all the ways we echo forward and back, our way of assuring one another: *We'll be back for you!* Our way of reminding ourselves that we are cherished. We are here for a time, but we are also wanted elsewhere.

In the weeks before my family and I depart New Jersey for Massachusetts, I am startled from sleep by a dream in which we have already embarked on the journey north. In the dream, my husband sits at the wheel. Our headlights illuminate a four-lane highway that stretches hundreds of miles.

Abruptly, my perspective shifts. I've been lifted from the passenger seat. Strapped to the outside of a massive vehicle, the kind designed to transport large sheets of glass. I am pinned down by the arms of a rack meant for holding the fragile plates in place. Padlocked at the breastbone and between my hips. This vessel, the size of a semi, is loaded with Black women and men, rounded up, like me, in the course of a normal night. We've been left with nothing. Even our legs have been stripped bare. I peer down at my family's car, pulled to the side of the road, idling. My children remain buckled in their seats. My panicked husband paces the shoulder. The massive semi engine growls, turning over.

It's the only time I've dreamed of the Middle Passage.

The dream reminds me that I am afraid. I do not want the life I sail toward to be worse than the life I leave behind. The dream also allows me to acknowledge the inevitable loss that accompanies departure. That panic in my chest, the creak of those metal racks, the hiss of traffic rushing past: a nightmare like this reminds me that even at a time of choice, a time of thanks and praise for good fortune, I remain afraid for something as elemental as my safety and the sanctity of my family. And that this fear extends from history.

As a child when I'd wake, crying, from a nightmare, my mother was there to assure me everything was okay. We'd pray for peace of mind, calm of spirit. Then she'd tell me to roll over onto my other side, or shift the position of my arms and legs, so that the pattern of the night-mare would be disrupted.

It is a different day. The fright of that dream has faded. But the world is full of patterns that devastate me, and so I sit on my couch to meditate. I lean back and cover myself with a quilt. I close my eyes. I enter the rhythm of breathing. Gradually, there is the sense of depth, a farther field aswirl with ashen dust, against which the shape of a black mountain range is defined. *I've arrived,* I think to myself, as if the journey has been arduous, as if there is some exhaustion I must be seeking to appease with the good news that there is no further distance left to cross.

Those dark human silhouettes? The ones that arrive in meditations like these? I am met by a forest of them. They rise as if from the ground, as if they have been congregated here together resting, or working at something close to the soil. They grow tall and draw near. My body—I can feel it there on my couch, in my house, where it is propped on pillows and warm under the weight of a quilt—my body rests at ease, safe at home, while the soul of me roams.

When I tell the familiar figures what I need—assurance, peace of mind, courage, and strength—do you know what they do? One by one they climb down into me. Down, because I am reclining there like a low boat before them. They flood in.

The quiet channels of water and the reeds growing up through mud are like the labyrinthine waterways where rice grows, or once grew. Perhaps rice is something the tall forest of figures here knows, or once knew. But there is no hurry. No sun to get out from under. No winter about to descend. Nothing follows on our heels. Nothing sighs waiting for us to arrive. Nothing hollers out impatient from the banks. Nothing scolds. And yet, I believe that some labor awaits, that they are here to reveal a task not yet complete.

I drag my hand through the water. Shallow runnels swell up and pucker the smooth glassy surface we skim. The air is still. The boatman's shoulders and arms move in a rhythm I teach myself to breathe to. Purposeful unhurried strokes. Have I asked him to lead? Have I asked to be led? From where I am, behind him and below, my eyes can't graze his face, which anyway would be a soft unfeatured plane not clearly seen. He doesn't need to be held, caught, claimed by my gaze. He is his own. This goes for the others, too, even the ones I somehow carry.

It's a late spring morning, and I am at the Ogden Museum of Southern Art in New Orleans. I was here yesterday as well, feeling nourished by the work of artist RaMell Ross—assured that family is any group of people with whom you share history. The promise and the challenge of that fact. Today, I find myself in thrall to a photograph entitled *The Gotten Tree*. An image of a young Black man who stands in the center of a road, bent at the waist over a fallen tree. As if he seeks to push or drag or somehow resurrect the dark body.

Alone in the gallery and in this city, a nearly thirty-year-old memory floods me:

My first visit to New Orleans was to attend a reunion on my mother's side of the family in 1995, the summer after my mother's passing. I stayed in her brother's grand house. I swam in his pool. I paraded with my cousins through the French Quarter. One night, my uncles drove all of us nieces and nephews out to the bayou, where we parked in the grass by the side of the road and shone flashlights into the dark. *A gator's eyes'll shine back red at night,* they told us. What were we doing out in that dark swampy grass? We laughed and laughed. I ate a thigh of fried chicken wrapped in white sandwich bread. We made too much noise. Sometimes something living was almost caught in our jittery beams.

After so much nonsense, after so much revelry, on the night of the reunion banquet, I was overtaken by resentment. I refused to smile. I scowled in every photo. Suddenly I needed to punish someone, everyone, because my mother was gone. As if my aunts and uncles, my mother's dozen surviving siblings, weren't also grieving.

Decades ago now, the contusion of that season returns. The play and ease of my uncles. The proud strength of my aunts. The way the tall trees and wide sky let me feel large for a time, broken and angry though I was. And how it had surprised me to feel large in the South, where I had naïvely expected everything would be seeking to cut me down.

I'm almost the age of my mother when she left us. In gratitude for her life, and for my living, I send a piece of myself into each photograph in the gallery. An offering. Here, on a rain-wet road. There, in tall grass. Lying still beside that woman on the dappled daylit porch.

In the image that most captivates me, the young man bends at the waist above a fallen tree. His whole body is coiled with potential energy. He reminds me of those cowboys who seem to hold themselves in the air above the seat of the saddle as their horses gallop forward or rear up, the ones whose lassos stencil shapes in clear blue unparcelled sky—

Because the first American cowboys were Black men.

After emancipation, they hired themselves out to do the work they'd been born or sold into. Not cattle herds, not ranch hands; those were jobs for white men. Cowboys. Cow boys. Black men on horseback kicking up dust, whipping lariat loops into crisp air, whistling and singing across the vast lonely plain. Bill Pickett, credited for inventing bulldogging: the sport of wrangling a steer to the ground by the horns. Nat Love, also known as Deadwood Dick, who married and eventually settled into a career as a Pullman porter (another kind of traveling hero). Bass Reeves, who escaped slavery during the Civil War and became the first Black deputy west of the Mississippi. I believe it is owing to the legends of men like these that my father kept a cowboy hat and a long leather-collared duster, and made passing reference sometimes to the rifle he owned and knew how to handle. Reeves was a master marksman. He's said to have been the inspiration for the Lone Ranger—though you can be sure this theory is contested. The only part of Reeves ever grazed by a bullet, so the story goes, was his hat. Imagine. Black men high up on horses, belts slung with guns, their very silhouettes against sunset shorthand for freedom. White men, wanting that valor for themselves, decided to put the Lone Ranger in a mask, to take away the face altogether. They remade him as mystery, mythology. To mythologize is to lift out of history.

When the Texas frontier was settled, free whites (some were slaveholders) carved communities from the grazing habitats for bison, an animal crucial to Comanche survival. As settler populations ballooned, Comanche hunting grounds were whittled into an ever-dwindling margin, and the bison began to be pushed to near extinction. This pattern of encroachment, removal, and erasure—we might more honestly call it a *strategy*—recurs throughout colonial history and Westward Expansion in the United States. Comanche raids were a means of defense against the violence of settler colonialism. These acts were not merely *warlike* (the Comanche are almost always described as *warlike*), they were acts of armed retaliation in what American history has named the Indian Wars.

The cowboy Britt Johnson rose to the position of foreman on the Texas ranch where he was enslaved. By all accounts, it was his loyalty that earned him his own horses and herd of cattle—though I want to believe such a circumstance was owing at least equally to his expertise. On October 3, 1864, while Johnson was away from home, his son, Jim, was one of a dozen people massacred in the Elm Creek Comanche Raid. His wife, Mary, and their two daughters, Jube and Cherry, were kidnapped. Neighboring farms were destroyed. Every horse, every head of cattle was stampeded away.

Johnson's months-long quest to find Mary and their daughters, which resulted in his surviving family being reunited in the spring of 1865, became famous. His story was the inspiration for the character Ethan Edwards in Alan Le May's 1954 novel *The Searchers*. In John Ford's 1956 film of the same title, Edwards—Uncle Ethan—is played terrifyingly by John Wayne, who searches for his niece Debbie for years following a raid similar to the one that claimed young Jim Johnson's life.

I wonder if all John Wayne's characters combined to become the man or the men we think of as Wayne himself, the man he was eventually presumed (or perhaps required) to become, or appear to become. Isn't Wayne part of the myth of the cowboy? Quiet but for that halting singsong speech. Feelings swallowed down fathoms deep, out of reach. Slow walk. Quick draw. When Ethan finally finds his niece—when he can see that she is now truly a Comanche, that she speaks the language just like they do, and has taken on their garb, their manner (he must wonder what else she has accepted), when she says in English, *These are my people*—that's when he reaches for his pistol. You can see it dawning in his face the whole time—the way his eyes squint to take her in, then spit her back as though she is flesh and nothing more—damaged, dirtied, nullified of all worth by her by now willing proximity to the Comanche.

Stand aside! Wayne shouts to his nephew Martin, who attempts to shield his younger sister with his own body. *Stand aside!*

It is impossible for me to reconcile Johnson's original quest for his kin with the cold vendetta enacted by Wayne on the wide Technicolor screen. In my mind's eye, Johnson wanted what countless other Blacks sought as soon as they had autonomy over their lives: to bring family back together intact and alive. To close the circle. To free the captives.

Johnson's quest brings to mind the thousands of nineteenth-century newspaper notices appealing to readers across the nation for help locating longed-for kin:

> *Information wanted of my son, Allen Jones. He left me before the war, in Mississippi. He wrote me a letter in 1853 in which letter he said that he was sold to the highest bidder, a gentleman in Charleston, S.C. Nancy Jones, his mother, would like to know the whereabouts of the above named person . . .*

and:

> *I have somewhere in Virginia two brothers and one sister. Their names are Nick Sanders, Nussua Sanders and Sookie Toles. My brother Uriah and I were sold from Lancaster County about 45 years ago at the sale of old Mrs. Polly Cavern. My father, Abraham Sanders belonged to Joseph C Cavern, and after his death his wife sold us out. I have an aunt; her name is Matilda Woods and a friend Sam Lonely and his family.*

He knew my father, Abraham Sanders, he lived next door to us.

Any one that knows anything about any of the above named parties will confer a great favor by writing me . . .

and:

PLEASE HELP ME FIND MY BROTHER

Saunk Joyce was sold in Mecklenburg, Virginia several years before the civil war, to Cunnigan a Negro trader. His mother, Willie, was a slave on the Joyce plantation. He had one sister Betty, who is very anxious to find him. Any information will be gladly received . . .

A decade after my first visit to New Orleans, over the July Fourth weekend in 2005, my mother's surviving siblings, her four brothers and eight sisters, along with their children and their children's children—all of us gather. We move between my uncle's house in New Orleans, his ranch in Mississippi, and the siblings' child-hood home in Alabama. Two of these states, Alabama and Mississippi, are as far back as we can with certainty trace our own ancestry. Some of my mother's siblings have already begun the reverse migration back South and now live nearby, an hour's or a few hours' drive. For a few hot summer days, we are all within reach.

My first morning waking up here, I'm drawn outside by the layer of fog kissing the surface of a pond on my uncle's land. That water—placid, dark as fallen leaves, and who knows how deep—it strikes me not just as a happenstance feature of the place; it suggests a kind of circumstance. I am one of those people who reads too much into the landscape of the South. I expect always a chorus of voices calling out in knowledge, in admonition. All the moss draping the branches of trees says, *Imagine what we've seen.* The scarified trunks of live oaks repeat the same. And why call a tree *live* if death is not somehow a topic of consideration? A certain quantity of this is my own seeking. *I know what happened here* is the statement I feel thrumming in my pulse, like a spell that might keep me from being caught and held. But do I know? Is this summation, and the fear that fuels it, any different from what, in another imagination, might manifest as nostalgia, a way of seeking to participate in a past that, for whatever reason, beckons still? The placid glassy water. Muscled moss-slung trees. What should seek to hold me here if not the part of myself most drawn to the things I command myself to fear?

One of my mother's brothers rides up on a horse. As much as I know they come from farmers—cotton and pine, but also hogs and horses, mules and cows—I have not thought to imagine my uncles can do this, that they can *still* do this. But his body knows what it knows. The animal is steady, graceful, and my uncle's bearing betrays no fear. Not a sliver of him says what my body has always said the handful of times it's been entrusted to a saddle: *What am I doing here?*

My cousin follows. A cousin I always think of as a little big-toothed boy because that's what he was, way back when we first met. Here he is now on his own horse, knowing exactly what to do with the reins and the stirrups, shifting his weight with the horse's gait. He's indisputably a man, taller and broader, too, than most all of our uncles, whom age has begun to make small. Soon, I will encounter Kehinde Wiley's paintings for the first time in a museum gallery. I will stand looking up at men like these—men like my young cousin has become—mounted high on steeds like gods, like angels, like kings. And it will be the exact same awe escaping my lips here in Mississippi that returns again then, familiar to me.

On the morning of the Fourth, preparations ensue for a massive crab boil. A large rectangular tent is spiked and filled with banquet tables. Caterers arrive with cauldrons of corn, crawdads, and crabs, and barrels for stripped husks, empty shells, and sopping paper trash. You spread it all out on the table, you revel in the abandon of the picking and the sucking. The paper bibs some wear are mostly a means of granting everyone permission to have at it, to feast like children, to imagine a time when nobody was watching.

I am captivated by my uncle's friends. Black men in ten-gallon hats and boots. One even wears real chaps. They ride in on their own thoroughbreds and quarter horses. I learn the terminology: a thoroughbred is a distinct breed, spirited and lively. You've got to know what you're doing to ride one, and not just anyone can break one in. *You have to be a real cowboy,* laughs one of my uncle's friends, flashing a wide grin. A quarter horse is easier-going, a cross between a mustang and a Chickasaw horse. *Chickasaw.* This word stirs up the remembered rumor that there is Choctaw and Chickasaw heritage somewhere in our family, something an uncle once set out to explain when several of us were together and the conversation had meandered around to history, which it inevitably does, history being memory. The lineage may trace back to the time when both tribes were slaveholding nations. It may also be owing to our family's Mississippi heritage and the few thousand Choctaws who managed to remain in that state even after the forced removal of the majority of the tribal nation.

Once or twice when I asked my father about this possibility, about his own mother's long black braid, he
answered back, shaking his head, *We're thoroughbreds.*
He'd done the hard work his whole life of defending his
dignity as a Black man. He'd taught us to do the same
as Black children. He refused to undermine this effort
by claiming some other lineage, which perhaps would
have represented, at another time, an escape hatch from
identification with Blackness. Understanding the reason for my father's refusal stopped me from pursuing
the question further.

I have been listening for some time, and with visible
rapture, to my uncle's friend's explanation about what
it means, today, to call oneself a cowboy. It is a con-
tinuation of a spirit and an occupation that has always
been, at least that's what he tells me. It's about dignity,
self-sufficiency, courage. The freedom he describes is
different from what the cowboy's mythology has taught
me to believe. It's not about disappearing from something, riding off into a duty-absolving sunset. It's about
standing up, shouldering a responsibility to self and
land and family that weighs differently, owing to how
much has sought to withhold from you the opportunity
for these very things.

His Nokia rings. It's clipped to his belt, and he
answers on speaker.

I'm looking dead at you, says a woman's voice. I hear

her twice: through the phone and in person from a few feet away where she stands—feet planted wide, weight to one side, one hand on a hip, and with a big angry smile—as if she wouldn't mind a fight.

I'm looking dead at you, too, he laughs back to his girlfriend or wife. His laughter skips toward her like a stone, sharp and flat.

I can feel the blade of her gaze as she eyes me, misreading my intentions. Though I'm sure she knows her cowboy.

When I am eventually offered the chance to ride, it's almost dusk. My boy cousins, who are not anymore boys but men, have gathered on the periphery, saddled up, going somewhere together like a magnificent posse. Part of this holiday is, for me, about feeling the presence, by way of the absence, of my mother. Here in the gloaming with so much kin towering above the ground like centaurs or warriors, it seems that rather than drawing my mother toward us, we have been allowed to follow her some few paces toward the otherworld.

I am instructed to place my left foot into the stirrup. Someone's firm hand helps steady me as I lift myself and swing the right leg over the saddle. And then a few firecrackers go off in the brush. Little kids, likely. But the horse skitters. Is it a thoroughbred? I hold on tight, waiting for the animal to settle. *Get down,* mouths my sister Jean from a distance. *I'm trying,* I mouth back, not knowing how to dismount while the animal skips forward and back, left and right, wheeling around in the first stage of its fright. When I look down again, the cowboy's girlfriend is there below me.

That's my man, she says, nodding over toward the cowboy. *And that's my horse.* She points to the animal I cannot quite rightly be said to ride. *Now you get down off of that horse.*

Briefly what flashes in my mind is the scene in Nicholas Ray's film *Johnny Guitar* where Mercedes McCambridge stands exulting, desperate for blood, imploring anyone, anyone at all to whip the horse on which Joan Crawford has been balanced, hands tied, neck draped in a noose.

My cousin steadies the mare, leans me down from the saddle like a child. I walk, trembling, back over to the tent. Frightened and alive.

A day later, we're in Alabama, at what we still call Mother's House. Though she hadn't lived there for some years, Mother—my grandmother—passed only a little over a year ago. It's still too soon to call this house anything but hers. In fact, it always will be Mother's House.

We sit outside in the yard at morning, my aunts and an uncle, my sisters, my brothers' wives and their kids. The air is heavy with moisture. The land is a rich oxidized red, but instead of the iron and coal reserves buried in this part of the earth, I think of the deep rich warm red brown hue of our skin in sun. This was my mother's home. And Sunflower is minutes away. My young parents ran shoeless on these dirt paths, drove grooves into mud. I can imagine their young hopes tethered to the stars in these wide-open skies. It's a backward-facing thought, a way of giving thanks for my mother, who walked the earth once. And my father, too, who walks it still in the summer of 2005, though the South, he protests, is not his favorite place to visit in July.

I am filled with love for my aunts' feet, set down on top of their shoes so they might be barefoot outside without tracking dust back indoors. One foot cradling the other, toes fanned out in pleasure. Later, we take pictures of one another posing on the hood of an old Pontiac. Chest up, toes pointed, one leg stretched straight, I mimic the silhouette on every big rig's mudflaps, but my mother's youngest sister, looking teasingly at the camera from over her shoulder, is the clear winner.

Age is erased. My aunts, my cousins, even the little baby cousins running around underfoot—we are all one. This is what kin means. A single fabric, warp indistinguishable from weft. I'm not sure if it is because I know I'll be flying home soon, or if the cause is something else, but I understand that we are huge inside the feeling we together constitute. Time stays back. I cease to worry about what the trees, only two days ago, seemed so eager to remind me. I listen instead to our voices, the engine of our laughter. At night, our patter is buoyed by crickets, katydids, singing frogs.

There is a little cousin, a baby boy three or four years old, whom I've fallen in love with. For as long as he'll let me, I carry him in my arms, breathe in the tender smell of his hair, doze on the couch with him flopped on my chest like a doll. *One day I'll have a baby of my own,* holding him causes me to hope. When he stirs, I cradle his neck until he settles. When he wakes, and runs outside barefoot into the night, I surrender him to the rest of us.

My brother and niece want to go off toward the woods and look for things. When she invites our little cousin to join them, he looks at her like she's crazy.

There's snakes in the woods, he says.

My dad is coming with us, we'll be okay, she assures him, unperturbed.

Maybe she has never really intended to leave the circle we make. Maybe we're all just about ready to go back inside anyway to play cards around the table and pull out the leftovers from just a few hours ago.

There's bears in the woods, our baby cousin warns.

A hurricane will threaten to touch ground here before we can fly home. We'll hunker down together under the lash of wind and rain. In another month's time, Hurricane Katrina will arrive as if to upend history. But in the moment, all I can inhabit is this night, when I feel glad knowing our baby cousin knows what anyone ought to know about living here. About snakes and bears and woods.

....

But because something is always watching, always circling, often veering in close to sniff before loping off again for a time into the distance, I'll return to history, to a gathering of a different tenor.

This story is about a boat with bodies in its hold. A boat called the *Clotilda,* sailed in 1860 from Mobile, Alabama, to the Dahomey Kingdom of Wydah, in what is today Benin, West Africa. Sailed there and back in the fashion of other such boats, galleons with peculiar names:

Antelope.
Juno.
Volunteer.
Spy.

Jamaica Packet.
Two Brothers.
Baltimore.
Fly.

Planter.
Indian Prince.
Africa.
Success.

I'll tell it in broad strokes. I'm sick of stories like this, and there are so many submerged still, waiting for the waters to recede, waiting to be properly believed.

The *Clotilda* grazed the coast of Florida, cut east through the Caribbean, then southeast farther still until, after ten weeks at sea, the anchor was dropped in the Bight of Benin and the crew scuttled off after plunder.

One hundred and ten shackled men and women and children were hauled aboard and lodged below, the way—with a good shove—a splinter can be lodged where it does not belong and thus rendered painful and difficult to extract.

The white wake of that ship, at its good clip and chased by wind, churned and hacked and slapped and marked the surface of the water. And what I need you to remember is that that water made its way, over time, to mingle with other water. Every wake, every ripple, every burble of surf. The entirety of all past and future sea.

Timothy Meaher, the ship's owner, sat at home rubbing his hands together. His endeavor is sometimes described as a wager, a rich man's joke. Told this way, he becomes the kind of child wealth allows some to remain, a boy puffed up in a waistcoat and starched collar seeking attention, and more. I can see him saying *Place your wager!* to anyone who scoffed that it couldn't be done, that no man could revive the transatlantic slave trade, not half a century after law prohibited the importation of enslaved Africans (that is not what he called them) to these shores. Did anyone suggest that, possible or not, it was an abominable thing to do? If so, Meaher merely brushed them off with big talk about how he could get away with anything.

If freedom is worth amassing, a man like Meaher thought, it must occasionally be tasted, flaunted, proved. Otherwise, what does it matter? Otherwise, what is its use?

The 109 surviving men, women, and children of the 110 shackled and shoved onto the *Clotilda*—the ones hauled as if across a chasm of half a century—we might agree to deem them the first known time travelers. And like all time travelers, they wanted to go home. They remembered home. They asked to be returned. Home dwelt inside the word they called themselves: *Dahomey*.

War came. They were freed. The land they bought and town they built is called Africatown. It sits north of Mobile Bay. They raised houses. They loved. They planted stories in their children, and the stories sent out strong roots. Stronger than what threatened them if they uttered what they knew. They suffered disregard, and worse. The land bordering their community has been polluted for generations by industries that turn a steep profit. Many have died as a result. Those who survive are victors of nothing shy of war. That is what the guilty and the complicit have labored to wage, in Africatown and elsewhere. A war fought with:

rope—
guns—
doubt—
drought—
law—
land—
mobs—
dogs—
red lines drawn on maps—
memes—
spoofs—
silence—
indifference—
words—
theft—
jokes—
threats—
flood—
taxes—

levees—
lies—
pride—
scorn—
ash—
bronze—
snub—
bomb—
storm—
hail—
bail—
rigamarole—

Is there anything that hasn't been rendered a weapon? Even 1,300 acres of the Meahers' remaining undeveloped land, gifted to the people of Alabama as a state park, in an act of intended absolution that withholds all promise or hint of apology (*What did we do to deserve this?*)—even this takes on the contours of a weapon.

Oh, My Country! Won't you admit, can't you see that the white wake of the *Clotilda* has dispersed everywhere? Sloshed to the ocean, swept to the clouds. I am sipping it now from a glass. Is there yet a chance that certain words, uttered in the right way, will land? And detonate?

Any information will be gladly received . . .

A video is sent to me via text one morning by a friend. An old friend whom I love. And because he wants me to have it, I sit and receive what I understand to be a gift.

It opens to one woman in a tight vertical frame, eyelashes like palm fronds, the hair at the top of her crown pulled up and left to waterfall down.

Listen, she says over the banter in the background. *This is my type of Mama's singing. She'll go . . . Let me find her key first. She'll be like—*

If the wind never quit blowing
Oh if the gray clouds always covered the sky
and oh if the billows never quit rolling
and it rain-rain-rained all the time—

The woman in-frame sings while her sister with the wavy strawberry blond locks stands behind, clipping the flowing black-brown tracks of a weave into the singing sister's hair. She clips and smooths, peppering the verse like a choir member in a church, singing along, backing the lead, stepping out of the song here and there to testify, *Yep, that's right! Uh-huh. Sing it high!*

The song continues on in the first sister's voice. She is faithful to the text, unrushed, singing out from the diaphragm as if trained. Both daughters have a performer's presence and poise. They have the type of voice we were deprived of, my sisters and I. Our mother, too, bemoaned her voice, a slight thing with hardly a range. She wanted to fill rooms with her praise! She'd have sat there just like the mother in this video whose daughters hover beside her, sifting hair, lifting their voices into the air like ether, then spreading them out low like valley fog. My poor sisters and I could have tended anything with such singing—any burden, any mood. That's what I tell myself even still, holding in the song that dwells in my own throat, keeping it close, not wanting its flaws to travel out.

Where are they? Who are they, the women in this family who sing without apprehension or error, striking their notes, meting their breaths, carrying their pleasure up beautifully into audible range, building something for others to enter? I enter there, though I am only really here, watching from my chair, peering into my screen at the room where the first sister is still singing—

And oh if the moon decided not to shine
and oh if the stars would never ever give a twilight
Lord, you gave me, oh you gave me
one more sunny day.

The camera shifts back to gather Mama, sitting on a bench at the foot of a bed. They are three women in a bedroom together singing and doing hair. There are bags and individual long dark locks laid out on the bedspread. A framed poster of the Eiffel Tower at night is centered on the far wall. A ceiling fan's white light bobs in and out of frame overhead, like a gibbous moon passing in and out of clouds.

Come on, Mama. The dark-haired sister has parted the water, and now she asks to be followed. Maybe she has always all along been only opening a path for their mother to enter.

And their mother is ready. She has been listening, letting something gather. She comes in in time to preface the next verse with a long sonorous *Ohhh,* as if to ready the air for the true onset of her voice—

I said if the wind never quit blowing
And oh if the gray clouds covered the sky
And oh if the billows never quit rolling
and it rain-rain-rained all the time.

The camera pans quickly again to the sisters, each blinking out from behind a thick fringe of lash, then back to Mama where she sits and sings. The standing sister proceeds with the weave up toward the top of the seated sister's crown. She warns, *Mama, you better get ready to come here.* Her turn in the chair is next.

Their spontaneous joy reminds me of one evening years ago when our sister Wanda, who is the oldest and was living farthest from home at the time, sat up all night talking by the fire with Jean and me in our family home. We told stories. We laughed. Our mother used to say that often there is discord within a group of three; that it's easy for two to pair up and for the remaining one to feel left out. But that night we operated symmetrically. We sat by the fire so happily for so long it made sense to stay. We didn't want the moment to go away. So we pulled out quilts. We spread ourselves on the rug. We told and asked things even sisters sometimes forget to share. That was the night I learned that Wanda, like me, bobs her right foot up and down from the ankle, as if operating a sewing machine pedal, while falling asleep. Small things like that. Things you nevertheless never forget.

That's it, the sisters say.

Come in, Mama, they coax.

Tell me that story, they offer.

That's it, they affirm.

Come on, tell the story.

Sing the song, now!

Meaning: *Let it out, let it all out. Let us help you. We're with you. We're here. We're ready. Take us. Take us with you.*

I got alto, says the standing sister before the two

launch into harmony. They let their mother lie back awhile and just comp, dispensing with the long lines and dropping in only a word or two at a time. The daughters clap like a choir, elongating, repeating, bending time. This is another way to tell a story.

Mama's arms preach. Her head tilts up toward God, then back to us. She is thanking Him. He's been good, He's been kind, she wants to thank Him, yes she does . . .

What is a billow? I finally think to wonder. I learn that it is *a large undulating mass, typically cloud or steam.* A billow is what billows in to smoke or choke us out. A billow can fill your chest sometimes, can rush your eyes, can make it so you have to get down on your belly with your chin to the floor if only to breathe. The song asks me to imagine, what if the billows rolled only in and in? What would it mean, even then, still to give praise, to nevertheless keep on offering thanks?

My mother did, in that last year of her life, after the end of her miracle, after the grace of her remission. A period in which the human part of her began to grow small. Every morning, every night, there in her bed, praising God, thanking Him, though the billows, her cancer, rolled ever in.

We sang for her once. It was nothing like these sisters singing here. Not a miracle of tone or timing and breath. Our singing was love's chore, knowing how we sounded but pushing the songs forward: *This little light of mine, I'm gonna let it shine* . . . We eked it out at her request, hoary and off-key like a stage whisper. She wanted church songs, familiar hymns, just like in Sunday school:

> *What a friend we have in Jesus,*
> *All our sins and griefs to bear.*
> *What a privilege to carry*
> *Everything to God in prayer.*

Except as I sang, I harbored not gratitude but grief, bewilderment, my own young rage. It did not feel like a privilege to live waiting for loss to sweep in and snatch my mother away. Where was I? In her room? At the foot of her bed? And also at the end of the beginning of my life, not knowing what would follow. What could follow? Would God open a window? Would He barge in, throwing back the door?

What if the God the women in this video are singing praises to is the same God who left us, my whole family and me, to carry on living in this world we all know, where sometimes a gust might blow, yes. And other times the wind will stall, letting a low-pressure system billow and grow. Where we wait and hope and sometimes fall quiet and still, adapting to the close weight of inevitable loss, like smoke, like fog.

With their voices, the daughters cushion their mother. With their voices, they race ahead, fanning her. They follow behind, lifting the train of her song, which leaps forward in time, and leaps in verb tense, too, to remind us not what God may yet do, but what He did, what He once chose to do.

These daughters will not tell us in this moment, this document of a single evening, what specific burden has been overcome. Neither will this mother, this survivor, resting on a bench at the foot of her own bed. I wonder if I recognize as familiar some small piece of the great weight she's been allowed for a time to defy.

How small I feel, thinking it: *Something else will claim her. Something will come to claim us all.* But the song, their voices, the dark I can feel beyond the bedroom's far wall, the rhythm they make and keep, the place the song seems to lead, and how it could go on forever in verse upon verse upon verse, in chorus and bridge and languageless riff. *Look*, it all but commands. Not to us anymore, but to God. *Just look, at what You did, what You came here to do, even as You are also off ahead in the realm where loss and pain and even victory, too—where everything earthbound falls away:*

You gave me one more sunny day
You spoke to the clouds and they all passed away
You spoke to the wind and the four winds stood still

You spoke to the billows and they all obeyed your will
I got one more, one more day . . .
I got one more, one more day . . .
Yes one more. Just one . . .

This woman, this mother, was in it, she was under it. Yet she looks not forward but back. Tomorrow is outside of the song's final bars, which have been bent and stretched anyway to make space for more thanks. Tomorrow is another song, a different 'do, a matter of faith.

When the final verse is over, the standing sister with the pale wavy hair picks up a weave track, then thinks better, dropping it back down and prancing to the foot of the bed. If they were onstage, this is where the electric bass would kick in, and the horns and drums. Where the crowd would roar, and their billows of joy would race in and collect, would roll on and on in the voice of the sea. And who knows? Maybe the song would give way to something about hunger for an earthly love, about a paycheck on Friday and a new car. Maybe it would commence to wail about a different kind of scar. The standing sister conjures this feeling of a party just getting started as she high-steps to the empty part of the room.

They laugh, they squeal, they breathe out, they testify. Then the standing sister returns to her task. Her seated sister needs one more row, maybe two. And the mother's crown still remains to do.

In this day and time, you better thank Him! their mama says. She does not get up. She has finished the song, but basks in its wake.

My my my my my! Yes, honey, that's Mama, says the sister in the foreground with the long black-brown locks. *That's where we get it from.*

I don't know why I have been thinking this whole time that they are getting ready to go onstage, when they are clearly in a house, at home. When this is clearly not a performance; it is life itself. Most likely they are going downstairs to dinner, or to bed for the night. Or going, together or apart, simply back out onto the stage of life.

When I try to return, in meditation, to the realm of shadows and channels and reeds where I sailed in the boat of my body, the place configures itself differently.

The mountains in the distance are nearer this time in my mind's eye. Chalky in the darkness, and moon white.

I wait. I wonder what I will be permitted to see.

Liquid again. Dark waves of open sea. I stand near the prow of a ship, an ark. I am there among others. Beside and behind them, small in a forest of tall shoulders, long arms.

We list and tilt, lift and drop, tossed in the warring currents of a storm. This water is the totality of all waters. I've said as much, but now I see. Dark, muscled, and filled with our refusal, our insistence, our forgetting. We are the matter. We are the source of its unrest.

Those few who have greeted me, filled me, led me from the safety of another vision's quiet banks? Now they lead me to see where all are heading, where all will meet. Every *Us*, every *We*, every cherished familiar few. And they will not let me stop with them. There are none who do not number among us on this deck, among the generations of every known and chosen family. What each makes of the figures among us, and of what the churning waves lift for each into view, will, for a long time, appear to differ. But what surrounds us—the white wake of every ship that has churned up history—will break, eventually, around and upon us all. This is what they have brought us here to see. The enduring disseminating sea. Which we stare out onto from the human plane insisting we are not, all of us, aligned.

I wonder what farther shore we may hope to reach. I wonder whether and where we arrive.

Red dirt. Pine needles and leaves. Trucks and trailers nestled under trees. The steep peak of a church roof. A trailer's rusted eaves. Veins of road, like pale rope afloat on green sea. Railroad tracks running south, north, away. Dark water and a creek's muddy banks. The surface of the place shimmers in rain, shivers in wind.

And then, like a comet, he descends. He is born. He enters a room in the family home, is lifted into the arms of his mother, whom he has watched this long time as if through valley fog. He nuzzles in, and she peers down to breathe him in, cradling the soft wet curls on his head, the tantalizing nape.

His father is called in from work to meet the newest son, whose dark eyes seem to reach back far. He offers the baby a finger, which the boy grips. And *Look at that!* his father says. *See how strong he is?*

Soon he can run. Soon he can tell time. Soon he packs a bag and travels off into his life. Parts of them journey with him, through joy and wonder and loss, as they must. There is work ahead. Something must be seeded, tended, protected.

He lends his hands to the mammoth task. He teaches his children, too. They stand together at the forge, brothers, strangers, a lineage of souls, stretching forward and back for generations.

They crank the wheel that churns the bellows. In freedom and freedom's tall shadow.

In 2017, I give a poetry reading in Glasgow, Kentucky, a city of about 15,000 residents, the vast majority of them white. The event is hosted in an airy community center housing a museum of regional history. I arrive early to explore the large-scale dioramas of a settler house, country store, and schoolroom. I stand shoulder to shoulder with uniforms once belonging to local veterans of the Civil and World Wars, now buttoned onto department store mannequins. I skim educational resource materials that encourage school-aged visitors to write letters to family members as if they themselves have been sent off to war; to make lists of the modern-day tools that could have made life easier for members of the Shawnee, Cherokee, and Chickasaw— tribal nations referred to only as *Hunters and Gatherers in Kentucky.*

That evening, I read from a suite of my own poems curated from archival letters by Black soldiers of the

Civil War and their family members, as well as depositions given after the war by Black veterans petitioning the military for their rightful pensions. In many cases, these pleas persist, via widows and descendants, into the twentieth century. After my reading, a white woman approaches from the audience to say she was moved by the voices in the poems—and would I be willing to wait for her to hurry home and back for something she'd very much like me to have. There is plenty of time before the book-signing and reception are set to wind down. I assure the woman I'll do my best to wait.

But when she returns an hour later, the woman looks stricken. The voices in my poem had put her in mind of all the old folk songs her grandmother had once sung, songs this woman and her siblings had grown to love. In order not to lose them—and to hold on to the sound of a beloved family member's voice—they'd made a recording of their grandmother during the last years of her life. I notice that the whole time she relates this, the woman seems out of breath, as if she has run all the way there and back. But an hour has passed, more than enough time for her to get home and back. Something else has detained her.

I'm so sorry, she continues. *My grandmother would never have wanted to hurt you. But these songs— These songs—*

Of course. I've been slow to grasp it, but now I see the whole picture clearly before me. These songs. These old Kentucky songs. They're filled with notions and phrases certain to upset me. Things that will remind me of what a Black person would have been seen and labeled as by someone with no interest or belief in their humanity. I suppose this fact had never before occurred to this woman, who'd heard in these songs only the memory of her grandmother's childhood home, and the memories her grandmother had inherited from parents and grandparents of her own.

Each time I recall this encounter, it is with hope. It affirms that the patterns and even the assurances we've long clung to can be tempered and considered anew. Neither is it lost on me that this woman, after having arrived at a new private perspective on her grandmother's songs, felt that the experience would not be complete until she had returned to fulfill her duty to someone she'd likely never again see. She must have sat in her kitchen or living room or perhaps even her car listening again to her grandmother's voice, only this time with someone like me in mind. And this process, this happenstance, has somehow aided her grandmother in conveying, to her granddaughter standing before me, a message that might otherwise have gone unreceived: *I've been somewhere. I've seen something. It is time, finally, to remember different things.*

Where is the past? Behind us or up ahead? It is here. Beside us and within. Journeying through storm and din, and returning with news to everywhere we cast our attention.

ACKNOWLEDGMENTS

This book is an act of seeking instigated by the understanding that the losses we in our time are called to bear are great and increasing. But I believe there are things we know—and things we might muster the wherewithal to recollect—that will be of help. This is one attempt to know and to recollect.

Portions of this book, in early form, were presented at Grace Farms in New Canaan, Connecticut; as Harvard University's 2022 Alumni Day address; at Harvard's Mahindra Humanities Center; and as a fellow's talk at Harvard University's Hutchins Center for African & African American Research. Thanks for these opportunities are due to Kenyon Adams, Philip Lovejoy, Steven Biel, and Suzie Clark. And while thanks can't possibly encompass the awe, gratitude, joy, and affection I hold for my teacher, colleague, and friend Henry Louis Gates Jr., I offer it emphatically nonetheless.

At a dinner party in his home, Homi K. Bhabha discussed his own engagement with W. E. B. Du Bois's

Darkwater: Voices from Within the Veil, alerting me to Du Bois's elegant and incisive formulation for the nature of the affronts against which the Freed remain braced, referenced in my chapter "The Free and the Freed": "They do happen. Not all each day,—surely not. But now and then—now seldom; now, sudden; now after a week, now in a chain of awful minutes; not everywhere, but anywhere—in Boston, in Atlanta. That's the hell of it."

"Scenes from a Marriage, or: What Is the American Imagination," invokes Du Bois's concept of Double Consciousness and the "unasked question" hovering around Black experience in America: "How does it feel to be a problem?" defined in *The Souls of Black Folk.*

The James Baldwin quote appearing in "One More Sunny Day" is drawn from Baldwin's essay "My Dungeon Shook: Letter to my Nephew on the One Hundredth Anniversary of the Emancipation": "But these men are your brothers—your lost, younger brothers. And if the word integration means anything, this is what it means: that we, with love, shall force our brothers to see themselves as they are, to cease fleeing from reality and begin to change it."

Poetry is the system of inquiry and the tool of insight that has guided me more than any other, in this book and in life. And the great poet-ancestor Lucille Clifton is for me the model of the kind of light a poet might hope to receive and, in turn, impart. I am emboldened and affirmed by Clifton's belief in our ongoing dialogue with the cosmic beyond. The line "the lip of our understanding," referenced in "One More Sunny Day," comes from Clifton's poem "blessing the boats."

Certain passages in "One More Sunny Day" and "Sobriety" originated in episodes I authored for the MPR audio podcast *The Slowdown.* With special thanks to Tracy Mumford and Jennifer Lai.

Correspondence between Simon J. Tricksey Sr. and John H. Peach courtesy of Alabama Department of Archives and History.

David H. Onkst's scholarly article " 'First a Negro . . . Incidentally a Veteran': Black World War Two Veterans and the G.I. Bill of Rights in the Deep South, 1944–1948" was critical to my understanding of what the G.I. Bill did and did not provide for returning Black veterans like my uncles. It appears in the *Journal of Social History,* Vol. 31, No. 3 (Spring 1998): 517–43.

Visual images of history aided my ability to envision my own family members at different points in their lives. Ken Burns's 2007 documentary miniseries *The War* was helpful to my describing and imagining. *Detroit Free Press* photographer Tony Spina's 1953 photographs of Skid Row helped me visualize the Detroit my father would have encountered as a young man.

Last Seen: Finding Family After Slavery is an

online searchable database of ads posted by people seeking to reunite with family members from whom they were separated by the domestic slave trade: www.informationwanted.org.

Margaret Brown's 2022 documentary *Descendant* tells the story of Africatown, Alabama, and the community descending from the 110 people illegally abducted and enslaved aboard the *Clotilda*. The enterprise of freedom is bolstered by their ongoing efforts.

Tobbi White-Darks and Tommi White—the Gospel duo known as Tobbi and Tommi—are the sisters who join their mother in the soul-stirring performance of "One More Sunny Day" contemplated in "The Northern Territory."

Much of what has occurred to me here is the result of dialogue with guides and ancestors, peers, colleagues, family members, friends of my soul, and artists whose making and seeking have been sustaining, among them: Melissa McGill, David Semanki, Jean Smith, Richmond Smith, Ghyontonda Mota, Patrick Sylvain, Jericho Brown, Patrick Rosal, Linda Susan Jackson, Gregory Spears, Kevin Newbury, Markus Hoffmann, Erskine Clarke, Evans Mirageas, Bertha McKnight, Pat Bacote, and Jim Bacote, who has joined the ancestors. Also Su Hwang, Michael Kleber-Diggs, Douglas Kearney, Robin Coste Lewis, RaMell Ross, ZZ Packer, Kevin Young, Elizabeth Alexander, Aracelis Girmay, Jorie

Graham, Nii Ayikwei Parkes, Tina Chang, Robin Beth Schaer, Leila Ortiz, Rachel Eliza Griffiths, and our sister-ancestor Kamilah Aisha Moon. Thank you to my editor and friend John Freeman for inviting and emboldening me to write about these things in this way.

To Naomi, Atticus, and Sterling: thank you for filling my life with meaning, laughter, and love. And to Raphael, who read every draft of every essay, and spent whole seasons in dialogue with me about these chapters, many of which we lived together before the need to write about them arose: thank you for everything, always, all the time.

ILLUSTRATION CREDITS

13 Historical/Corbis Historical via Getty Images

14 Courtesy of The Mariners' Museum and Park,
Newport News, Virginia

15 Collection of Tracy K. Smith

17 Collection of the Smithsonian National Museum
of African American History and Culture

19 Collection of the Smithsonian National Museum
of African American History and Culture

21 Collection of the Smithsonian National Museum
of African American History and Culture

47 Collection of Tracy K. Smith

48 Collection of Tracy K. Smith

49 Collection of Tracy K. Smith

58 Collection of Tracy K. Smith

59 Collection of Tracy K. Smith

72 Collection of Tracy K. Smith

218 Collection of Tracy K. Smith

A NOTE ABOUT THE AUTHOR

Tracy K. Smith is the author of five acclaimed poetry collections, including *Life on Mars,* which was awarded the Pulitzer Prize; a memoir, *Ordinary Light,* which was a finalist for the National Book Award; and the original libretto for the opera *Castor and Patience.* From 2017 to 2019, she served as the twenty-second Poet Laureate of the United States. In 2021, she was named a Chancellor of the Academy of Poets. She is a professor of English and of African and African American Studies at Harvard University.

A NOTE ON THE TYPE

This book was set in a typeface named Bulmer. This distinguished letter is a replica of a type long famous in the history of English printing that was designed and cut by William Martin in about 1790 for William Bulmer of the Shakespeare Press. In design, it is all but a modern face, with vertical stress, sharp differentiation between the thick and thin strokes, and nearly flat serifs. The decorative italic shows the influence of Baskerville, as Martin was a pupil of John Baskerville's.

Composed by North Market Street Graphics
Lancaster, Pennsylvania

Printed and bound by Berryville Graphics
Berryville, Virginia

Book design by Pei Loi Koay